ORIENTED TO FAITH

WWW.ORIENTEDTOFAITH.COM

Oriented to Faith

Transforming the Conflict over Gay Relationships

by
Tim Otto

Foreword by
Shane Claiborne

CASCADE *Books* · Eugene, Oregon

ORIENTED TO FAITH
Transforming the Conflict over Gay Relationships

Cascade Books
An Imprint of Wipf and Stock Publishers
199 W. 8th Ave., Suite 3
Eugene, OR 97401

www.wipfandstock.com

ISBN 13: 978-1-62564-976-8

Cataloguing-in-Publication Data

Otto, Tim.

Oriented to faith : transforming the conflict over gay relationships / Tim Otto.

    xxii + 129 p. ; 23 cm. Includes bibliographical references.

    ISBN 13: 978-1-62564-976-8

    1. Homosexuality—Religious aspects—Christianity. 2. Sexual ethics—Biblical teach-
ing. 3. Christianity and politics. I. Title.

BR115.H6 O57 2014

Manufactured in the U.S.A.   06/27/2014

To my sister Nancy
who used her pain as a path to
empathy and love for others

*Let us then pursue
what makes for peace and
for mutual upbuilding.*

—ROMANS 14:19

Contents

Foreword

The gay issue is a divisive land mine that makes people angrier and more hostile than nearly any other issue. Conversations have become so unfruitful that some leaders argue we should take a vow of silence on the issue, at least for a season, as it does more damage than good.

Other folks are just exhausted by the debates around the seven passages[1] in the Bible that talk about "homosexuality"—so tired they won't even breach the issue with folks on the other side. We may "have good friends" who we disagree with, but we stay "friends" by avoiding this impossible issue.

So why in the world would you read this book?

Because Tim Otto is not interested in the gay "issue."

He is interested in God, love, community, justice, peace, reconciliation, grace, and Jesus—not to mention good Mexican molé recipes. He is interested in your story, your journey to God, and your quest for community, and he shares his story to help us all find a way forward.

Tim's story has the capacity to reshape the conversation because he makes the abstract personal, resurrects dead rhetoric, and puts a name and face to statistics or science or theology or whatever we think of when we talk about gay folks as "them" or "us" or "queer" or "sexual minorities."

I first met Tim at a festival on faith and justice. The organizers, though we did not all see eye-to-eye on same-sex relationships, decided to host a panel discussion on sexuality.

Each panelist was so fundamentally different that we wondered if there would be an awkward dissonance. One person was in a committed lifelong relationship with another person of the same sex and wanted to raise children and have a family. Another person was "ex-gay" and had participated in the

---

1. The seven passages are: Genesis 19:1–38, Leviticus 18:22 and 20:13, Judges 19:22–23, Romans 1:26–28, 1 Corinthians 6:9–11, and 1 Timothy 1:10.

Exodus International program designed to "pray away the gay" and "heal" people from same-sex attraction.[2]

Tears rolled as each panelist shared common threads of hatred, bullying, shame, exclusion, and though the panelists didn't all arrive at the same place—in fact, some seemed to arrive at very different places—all present witnessed the rare gift of a sacred, generative conversation about sexuality.

Tim's voice was—and continues to be—at the very heart of that conversation. He is confident in his identity as a gay man and a beloved child of God. He is proud of the community in San Francisco that has loved him over the decades and helped him to discern his path and vocation. He is humble—quick to listen, slow to argue—yet steadfast in what he knows to be true. He disarms you with his grace, wit, and gentleness.

In *Oriented to Faith*, Tim Otto offers us a beautiful chance to listen.

So often we think it is our job to push people to live a certain way, that the Spirit of God cannot convict hearts without our help. Billy Graham, when asked about the gay issue, said: "It's the Holy Spirit's job to convict, God's job to judge, and my job to love."[3]

Our friends at the Barna Group[4] conducted a study a few years ago in which they asked young non-Christians around the US about their perceptions of Christians.[5] The number one answer was: "anti-gay," then "judgmental," then "hypocritical" . . . and the list went on from there. Amongst this heartbreaking list of ugly things, "love"—the very thing Jesus said we will be known for—didn't appear. Nor did the fruits of the Spirit—kindness, goodness, joy, gentleness. As Christians, we have become known for those whom we have excluded, rather than those whom we have embraced. Regardless of your convictions on same-sex relations, we can all agree that if the number one perception of Christians is "anti-gay," we've done something wrong. Tim's voice can help us rediscover a Christianity that looks like Jesus again, when the world will know we are Christians by our love.

—Shane Claiborne

2. Over the past few years, organizers with Exodus have apologized for this posture and philosophy. The way evangelicals look at same-sex relationships is in flux right now, making this book very timely.

3. Quoted in Marin, *Love Is an Orientation*, 108.

4. A prominent research organization focused on the intersection of faith and culture.

5. Released as a book by Kinnaman and Lyons, *UnChristian*.

Preface

One of the scribes came near and heard them disputing with one another, and seeing that he answered them well, he asked him, "Which commandment is the first of all?" Jesus answered, "The first is, 'Hear, O Israel: the Lord our God, the Lord is one; you shall love the Lord your God with all your heart, and with all your soul, and with all your mind, and with all your strength.' The second is this, 'You shall love your neighbor as yourself.' There is no other commandment greater than these."

—MARK 12:28–31

One evening, sitting at a restaurant table with friends, I found myself on the receiving end of an angry lecture by a young woman whose goal was to help students at her seminary become more sensitive to gays and lesbians. I had admitted to her that I, a gay man, after years of diligently studying the issue, was sympathetic to both sides. But that wasn't an acceptable position to her. She declared that those who held the traditional view of homosexuality were God-damned oppressors, on the wrong side of the defining civil rights struggle of our time. And on she went, passionately insisting that her intention was sensitivity to gay people. I began to wonder whether I should say something rude to get her to stop.

In a seminary class called "Church and Ministry in the New Testament," I heard a pastor speak with heroic martyrdom of how he had split his church over the issue of homosexuality. When the question came up among his parishioners, he had "preached the Scripture," and in doing so had divided his congregation down the middle. After some drama he had resigned and then started a new church just blocks away. As he told it, 300 members of his former congregation "just showed up." "That is the cost you must sometimes pay when you preach the gospel," he said in summary to our class.

As I sat startled, sad, and angry that he had split his congregation, I wondered where was the call to love all of God's children as Christ loves them, including those of the Lesbian, Gay, Bisexual, and Transgender (LGBT) community. I struggled to put together a response in my head, but before I got my hand up, the professor thanked the pastor and changed the subject.

If this was "good news" (gospel), then the debate and division in the church over homosexuality—and not just one side of it—has a taken a very wrong turn.

A Third Way

Such extreme reactions are nothing extraordinary these days, and many Christians no longer believe it's possible to speak about homosexuality without drawing battle lines.

Yet there is a better way. I've seen it.

In 1988, when I was twenty-three years old and on the verge of giving up my faith, I made my way to San Francisco with knots in my stomach, anticipating a talk with my mentor, Jack Bernard. For me the controversy over homosexuality in the church was not an abstract debate, but a live question about how I was going to live my life. I had told a few people I was gay, but Jack was not among them.

At the time Jack was the area director for the Conservative Baptist Home Mission Society in the Northwest United States, and I wondered if he might give me a canned, party-line answer to my questions. But because I knew something of Jack's history, I had a slender hope he would do better.

Jack was the ace of all trades. He had been a pilot, a race car driver, an accomplished climber, skier, biker, and woodworker. When he became a Christian he set out to "ace" Christianity as well: he went to seminary and then became a missionary. But he quickly realized that in spite of his discipline and talents, he wasn't acing Christianity. He repeatedly set out with great resolve to "be a good Christian," but then would stall due to distractions with small things. This happened so often that he began to despair, not so much of God, but himself.

As he despaired of himself, he began to see his frantic efforts at achievement, "getting it right," and "making the grade" as his own efforts to be God and create his own salvation. He realized God was going to have to save him, and his own discipline, actions, and doctrines would always fall short. He had learned the way of faith, and because of that I trusted him.

Since I had last seen Jack, he and his wife had moved into a little Christian community among Salvadoran refugees in the Mission District of San

Francisco. I had arranged to live in the community for a time in order to sort out my life.

At one of the first community meetings, I gathered my courage and said, "I'm a Christian, and I'm gay, and I have no idea how those two things might go together. If possible I'd like to try to figure that out with you all." Though I felt suddenly naked, I also felt relief. Though people were surprised, they were also grateful for my openness. What Jack said afterwards is the basis for this entire book: "I don't know what to think about homosexuality, but by faith I suspect it is God's gift to you—and I know you are God's gift to us."

Introduction

"But the serpent said to the woman. 'You will not die; for God knows that when you eat of it your eyes will be opened, and you will be like God, knowing good and evil.'"

—GENESIS 3:4

Entering the Struggle

We are at a crucial point in the life of the church. As a community of believers, we must look through the lens of faith and ask the question, "What is God doing in all of us?"

We can fight one another while the world watches us with bemused cynicism, or we can discern how God is using our struggles to help the entire church become more faithful.

Regarding homosexuality, it is understandable that our first instinct is to determine and declare whether God thinks same-sex relationships are right or wrong. We are attempting to be good; we are trying to get it right.

People on the "traditional" side of the divide believe the historic teaching of the church: same-sex unions are wrong, for in the words of 1 Corinthians 6:9 (ESV), those who "practice homosexuality" will "not inherit the kingdom of God." Therefore, those who affirm gay unions are ignoring the plain sense of Scripture, and in doing so are endangering their own salvation as well as the salvation of others.[1]

People on the "affirming" side believe the overall story of Scripture points toward an ethic that celebrates same-sex unions. They are concerned that, like

---

1. I've struggled with what names to use for the two sides. For what it is worth, both the terms "traditionalist" and "affirming" have positive connotations for me.

the Pharisees of the first century, the traditionalists are reading Scripture in literalist ways that don't apply to people who have a natural and normal variation on human sexuality. For people on the affirming side, traditionalists, in the words of Matthew 23:4, "tie up heavy burdens, hard to bear, and lay them on the shoulders of others; but they themselves are unwilling to lift a finger to move them."

If either side can agree on anything, it is that the question of "right or wrong" is essential, and any other approach is a cowardly and harmful evasion.

But, to borrow a metaphor from Oliver O' Donovan, the "right or wrong" question may, like a breech birth, put the whole matter at the wrong angle.[2] We may need to turn the question before any helpful answer can be delivered.

At present, the church is bloodied and worn out from the internal war over this debate. Both the liberal and conservative sides of the church are inclined to write off the other. Our witness is in terrible disarray.

How Is God at Work?

Following Jack Bernard's example, rather than latching onto whether same-sex relationships are right or wrong, a better initial question might be: how is God working for the good? How is God working for the good through the controversy in the church around homosexuality? How is God working for the good through Christians who identify themselves as LGBT?

This approach puts faith first. The most fundamental marker of God's people is not that we are right about everything, but that we are a people who live by faith. As Genesis 3:4 suggests, Adam and Eve's sin was not that they chose evil in the place of good (at that point, they didn't know good from evil), but that they didn't trust God. Somehow, God was holding out on them, and this belief led them away from a trust in God to a desire to be little gods themselves, knowing good from evil.

By admitting we are fallen—that we are not little gods and our best reasoning about Scripture, tradition, and morality is human and fallible—we are free to trust God is with us, especially in the most difficult times. This allows us to recognize God is working all things for the good, even the struggle the church is facing regarding same-sex relationships.

The question, "how is God working for the good?" also helps us journey towards a more complete picture of God's will. Right or wrong questions can be answered by a single piece of knowledge. The question, "Is it okay to cross a street on a green light?" is useful because the answer may help us avoid terrible

2. O'Donovan, *Church in Crisis*, 5.

accidents. But just because we can cross the street safely does not mean we know where we are going. Obeying all the rules won't get us home. Asking, "how is God working for the good?" does not focus on a single piece of knowledge, but on our overall direction: "Which way is home, and what will it look like when we get there?" If we only focus on understanding the rules of the road, we will miss out on significant landmarks and obstacles and possibly never make it *home*.

Ultimately, recognizing how God is working for the good helps us pay attention to the real needs of people. The theologian and pastor, Dietrich Bonhoeffer, who was killed by the Nazis for his opposition to Hitler, wrote:

> Christ did not, like a moralist, love a theory of good, but He loved the real man. He was not, like a philosopher, interested in the "universally valid," but rather in that which is of help to the real and concrete human being.[3]

Wrestling towards Blessing

As John Howard Yoder writes, we "seek a truth system with which to defend ourselves as those who possess it, rather than being claimed by a Lord who calls us to join him in his condescension."[4] Like Christ, we must be willing to enter the struggles of faith and life alongside our brothers and sisters rather than simply making moral pronouncements on one another.

When I was a young man, I told an older Christian woman about my attraction to guys. She sat me down and carefully explained the dangers of rebellion. She pointed out the Scripture verses that condemn homosexuality. At the time, I believed she was probably right, yet I distrusted her instant diagnosis of me as rebellious simply because I was homosexual, and I disliked her dispensing verses like pills.

How unlike my experience with Jack, whose eyes sparkled with a curiosity that seemed to say, "I wonder what God is up to in Tim!" In that vulnerable moment, when I opened up to the community, Jack acknowledged the difficult ethical problem I presented, but saw me as a gift rather than a threat. As Jack and the community listened to me, accompanied me, and on occasion said very difficult things to me, I encountered the love and care of Jesus. At that crucial time, an opening appeared that has allowed me to walk forward in faith.

---

3. Bonhoeffer, *Ethics*, 85.

4. Yoder, *To Hear*, 64.

To see with the eyes of faith means that amidst difficulties, we believe we might learn something, and that as we struggle in faith, we may discover a blessing. If, as Tertullian said, even the devil is God's devil, then perhaps God is using our Christian brothers and sisters who disagree with us to teach us something.[5]

Regarding the controversy in the church over homosexuality, a charitable view of the traditional side is that it is concerned for righteousness and a charitable view of the affirming side is that it is concerned for justice. Interestingly, justice and righteousness are both possible translations for the same Greek and Hebrew words. As I've struggled with both sides for decades, I've come to believe both sides need each other in order for all of us to get closer to God's truth.

I'm writing this book because I have both conservative and liberal Christian friends, and I have seen something of what they have to offer each other. The fact that conservative Christians often feel closer to politically conservative non-Christians than to their liberal sisters and brothers in Christ, and vice-versa, makes me think we're all more immersed in worldly ways of reasoning than we are in the Christian story. Just as Scripture makes it clear that Jew and Gentile, male and female, slave and free are one in Christ, conservatives and liberals need to know one another as "one" in Christ.

By putting aside the question of "right and wrong," we can consider God's purpose for our sexuality without the pressure of coming to the "right" answer. Without this pressure, we can come closer to a truly Christian conversation on the topic, which I'll explore in chapter 9.

I'm not secretly trying to smuggle in a "God condemns" or "God affirms" same-sex relationships answer by asking, "How is God working for the good?" I promise I'm not going to "come out" with an answer to the morality question sometime later in the book. After hundreds, maybe thousands, of hours of reading, prayer, and conversation, I've come to believe that the central arguments of both the left and the right are based on the faulty story of the Enlightenment rather than the Christian story, which I will discuss further in chapters 11 and 12. Coming to a final "answer" as to the morality of same-sex unions is far more difficult than most of us imagine.

The fact that I'm not going to "come out" with an answer to the morality question later in this book may cause some of you to stop reading in frustration with my immoral lack of conviction (in either direction). I didn't write this book to change your view, but rather to consider how this debate might be an opportunity for the church to be transformed for the better, rather than flounder in an occasion for more division.

5. Apperson, *Wordsworth Dictionary,* 141.

Along these lines, I'd like to ask you to go through the difficulty of reading the chapters in this book that represent "the other side" for you as a way of listening to, and learning from, those with whom you disagree.

Odd, Generous Blessings to the World

The faith question will lead us into truth, a truth bigger than "right or wrong" judgments, a truth that requires costly changes in how we live. Flannery O'Connor is reported to have said, "You shall know the truth and the truth will make you odd."[6]

If Christians are going to make any kind of intelligible case one way or the other, we will need to form faith communities that demand far more of all Christians—communities that make us odd, generous blessings to the world. Much of this book will deal with how to form churches in which we love everyone—including gays and lesbians—better.

Forming better churches is crucial, because our Western culture deforms us. We need an alternative culture in which to live well. In chapters 3 through 8, I explain why our culture makes living a Christian sexual ethic something like trying to swim in thin air, and I suggest how the church can become water, where Christian living becomes more possible.

Beyond that, I hope this book helps you better interact with the people God brings into your life. Maybe you are a youth minister who recognizes one of your kids is gay or lesbian. Even if you are fairly confident you know the answer to whether God blesses or condemns same-sex relationships, I hope you will first ask, "What is God doing in this kid's life, and how do I cooperate with that?" Maybe you are in a denomination that is debating the ordination of gay or lesbian pastors. Perhaps you are firmly convinced of one side or the other. After reading this book, I hope you can better answer the question, "What is God doing in giving us this struggle?" Maybe you are gay or lesbian. By reading this book, I hope you can ask yourself, "What is God doing in giving this gift to me?"

Conservative readers may feel I've already reneged on my promise not to take sides. For if God only gives good gifts, how can something sinful be a gift? One way I've experienced homosexuality as a gift is that it has helped me see my need for God. A conservative perspective might agree with St. Thérèse of Lisieux's sister, Celine, who said, "I look upon all my imperfections as treasures, and I summon them to appear at my judgment, for all my faults are my strength. Since I regret them and am sincerely humiliated by them, I think

---

6. De La Torre, *Out of the Shadows,* 13.

that they will draw God's pity down upon me; and when he has pity, he also has mercy."[7]

Perhaps some of you already know what God is doing. Perhaps you are a traditionalist saying, "God is asking us to be holy and respect Scripture!" Perhaps you are an affirming person responding, "God has always been on the side of the oppressed; God wants us to do justice!" While there may be something to both of these perspectives, these quick answers are ways of conducting the same old arguments. Quick answers such as these place the "right or wrong" question in the primary position and then base the answer to, "What might God be doing?" on that.

A Difficult Curriculum

In this book I want to step back from the current debate and step out in faith that God is with us—right in the middle of our difficulty.

My friend Eric told me about one of his manic episodes. He hardly slept for weeks, bought hundreds of CDs, stalked a girl he was interested in, and alienated his pastor. Reflecting on all this, Eric realized his need for community and structure. He concluded his story by telling me, "God has given me a difficult curriculum." Eric chose to believe God had not abandoned him and was even using the difficulty of a manic episode to accomplish God's purposes in Eric's life.

I suspect in each of our lives there is a "difficult curriculum" that can either embitter us, or, if we choose the eyes of faith, can grow us into the people God intends us to be. I've experienced being gay as a difficult curriculum. But as "curriculum" implies, I've come to understand my attraction to men as a gift that has grown me, matured me, and helped me see truth I otherwise would have missed.

I think the church is in the same position. This controversy can amount to yet another sad chapter in the church's history of fighting and factionalism. Or we can realize that we have a tremendous opportunity in front of us and by exercising faith, we can grow because of God's goodness and grace. This book tries to spotlight God's grace by testifying how it has been at work in my own difficult curriculum, and how it might heal the church through the difficult curriculum facing us all.

---

7. Piat, *Céline, Sister Genevieve*, 151.

Questions for Discussion

1. Have you tried to talk with people who have a differing perspective on same-sex relationships? If so, what were those conversations like? What things made those conversations go well or go poorly?

2. The argument about homosexuality in the church is often focused on whether God affirms or condemns same-sex relationships. This introduction argues that a better question might be, "How is God working for the good in this controversy?" What kinds of answers can you imagine to that question?

3. Are there things in your life you can see as a difficult "curriculum?" If so, how is that change in perspective important?

1

·····································

Remembering Pain

"Tell me how much you know of the sufferings of others and I will tell you how much you have loved them."

—Helmut Thielicke

When I was six years old, I accepted Jesus into my heart. My parents were missionaries in Uganda, East Africa, and I would stand my mother's accordion case on end, open the family Bible on top of it, preach loud "sermons," and recruit a parent, pet, or peer to listen. Waving my arms flamboyantly and conducting hymns, I loved playing "church."

This was also the year I discovered the game "doctor." When other missionary kids would sleep over, I realized I had more interest in the bodies of the boys I explored than those of girls. Even at age six, playing "doctor" made me feel intensely ashamed.

In this chapter I'll try to relate what it was like to grow up gay. To understand homosexuality, in all its complexity, we must not speak in the abstract, but rather pay attention to particular people. As my mentor Jack taught me, paying attention to particular people might help us understand what God is doing here and now, among us.

Moreover, although same-sex attraction can be a helpful curriculum, it is important not to overlook the pain of growing up gay. An honest answer of how God is at work among us must take into account pain and difficulty. Of course I can't speak for all LGBT people, but I hope my story will help illustrate the kind of painful history that needs to be remembered.

Choice

As far as I can tell, I never consciously decided to be gay. The desires I experienced in myself shocked and shamed me. I didn't lie in bed as a six-year-old and wonder rebelliously, "How can I mess with my parents? Maybe I'll get a tattoo. No, too painful. Maybe I'll join a rock and roll band. And do what, play mom's accordion? I know . . . I'll be homosexual!"

When I was eight, the dictator Idi Amin kicked my family out of Uganda, and we returned to the United States. When I first came back, I knew I was attracted to boys, but I didn't have a name for it. I didn't think about it too much.

When I started school in California, I was called all kinds of names. Some names I could dismiss. Once I learned what the f-word meant, I thought about how "mother f-er" is inaccurate. "Well actually, I don't do that," I thought. But fourth-graders have amazingly good "gaydar." I got called names like "sissy," "faggot," "homo," "gay," and "queer" all the time. I began to realize, "Oh, those words actually apply to me." And so my peers taught me the words with which I would hate myself.

If there was any way I could have chosen differently, I would have. After having gone to fifteen schools by the time I was in the sixth grade (my parents, as missionaries, moved around a lot), I desperately wanted to fit in. I was uncoordinated, bookish, lonely, and beginning to develop pimples; the last thing I wanted was another way of being different.

A Life Paragraph

As I grew older I began to research sex and homosexuality by secretly reading the Christian books my parents had about sex. When I turned thirteen my parents bought me James Dobson's book *Preparing for Adolescence*. I devoured the book, and found its one short paragraph on homosexuality under the heading, "Questions of Fear." Question number nine is: "Wouldn't it be awful if I became a homosexual?" The book goes on to explain:

> A homosexual is someone who is not attracted to the opposite sex, but who is attracted to the *same* sex. It's a boy's interest in boys or a girl's interest in girls. Homosexuality is an abnormal desire that reflects deep problems, but it doesn't happen very often and it's not likely to happen to you.[1]

After the questions the chapter concludes this way:

---

1. Dobson, *Preparing for Adolescence*, 89.

Your sexual development is a normal event that is being controlled
inside your body. It will work out all right, so you can just relax and
let it happen. . . . If you can learn to channel your sexual impulses
the way God intended, this part of your nature can be one of the
most fascinating and wonderful aspects of your life, perhaps con-
tributing to a successful and happy marriage in the years ahead.[2]

While some people have a "life verse," I adopted those last sentences as my
"life paragraph."

I hoped my attraction to boys would be overcome if I channeled my
sexual impulses "the way God intended." I wasn't sure what that all meant, but
at least it meant "choosing" to be attracted to girls as much as I could. In junior
high I found myself vaguely attracted to a smart, articulate, athletic girl named
Elaine. She often wore a beret and dressed like a guy. I prayed my affection for
her would grow, and that somehow she might be interested in me. Later I realized I was interested in her because she was the most masculine girl I knew. In
college Elaine came out as a lesbian.

In junior high, I got beaten up regularly because I was "queer." Each day
I contemplated three separate ways home from school, and each one had its
share of bullies who would taunt and tease me, then beat me up. As the end
of the school day approached, nausea and dread filled my stomach as I played
Russian roulette route home.

Thankfully my family moved again when I began high school. Though
the bullying and name calling stopped, it continued in my head.

After an innocent thought like, "Ken has such beautiful green eyes," I
would think, "Tim, you are such a sick faggot." When I was honest with myself,
the word "handsome" seemed inadequate to describe some of the guys in high
school. They were achingly *beautiful* to me—both proof of God's existence and
of my own stench, weighing me down with shame and guilt.

In the early 1980s, there was very little awareness of LGBT students. I
didn't imagine there were any other students in my small-town high school
who were struggling with similar feelings. It was rumored that the drama
teacher was a "dyke," but that was said with scathing contempt. Gay jokes were
a constant part of joking between guys. As Brad East puts it, "To be gay was
the worst thing possible. To call another guy gay was the worst *insult* possible."[3]

I remember driving with my friend, Richard, by a restaurant that was
rumored to have a gay chef. Richard seemed to have everything going for him.
He was good-looking and artistic, he ran track, drove a hot car, and dated a

2. Ibid., 90.

3. East, "Friendship in a Fallen World," lines 60–61.

beautiful girl. Richard repeated the rumor about the gay chef and told me, "If I ever meet a homo I think I'll either run away or try to kill him."

Knowing Richard to be a better person than that, I still find it strange that he said what he did. But it reflected well the deep anxiety about homosexuality in that small town.

Knowing how my friends felt, and assuming I knew what my parents would think, I never told anyone I was attracted to guys. I tried as hard as I could to act straight and cover up any evidence of being gay. I wore flannel shirts and tried to learn a sport (tennis). I went on some dates with women, thinking if I went through the motions the feelings might follow. But the "fake it till ya make it" strategy never ended up working.

I believed if anyone knew I was attracted to guys, he or she would despise me. Believing I was fundamentally loathsome, I settled for what I unconsciously thought would be a substitute for love: admiration. I got good grades, won speech contests, and got elected junior class president and then student body president.

But the admiration I earned turned out to be shallow. As I stood in front of hundreds of students at pep rallies and games, I wished I could be with just one guy who knew all about me and loved me anyway.

Living the Victorious Christian Life

When I began applying to colleges, I told myself if I could be around more committed, loving Christians my life would be better, so I decided to go to a Christian college in southern California. My parents moved back to Uganda, and I drove down the I-5 freeway until I found the turn-off to my new life.

At first I thought Christian college was heaven, but I was still trying to achieve admiration through good grades. I had little time for friendships and didn't have the courage to tell others about my attraction to guys. The sunny campus culture dictated that being a good Christian meant living the "victorious Christian life."

Shame

For the summer, I fled the strip-malled, white, sterile, "courtesy capital of the world" for the streets of San Francisco. I knew some missionaries, Steve and Laura Reed, who worked with Salvadoran immigrants, and I joined Laura to work as a paralegal in her newly established law clinic.

I loved the colorful chaos of the Mission District, the aroma of carne asada burritos mingled with fresh fish markets and gutter garbage, the "painted lady" Victorians strutting their gaudy colors, the sound of Spanish and Cantonese and swear words and salsa music filling the air, the drug dealers and prostitutes and homeless and gang bangers who made the "fine" world feel fake, shallow, and distant. Some nights I literally skipped down the streets—knowing that skipping was "gay"—but in the anonymity and freedom of those streets, skipping was the perfect expression of the joy I felt.

One night, achingly curious, I walked into an adult bookstore. After looking at the gay magazines, I walked into the back where there were video-viewing booths for X-rated movies. Someone propositioned me, and we went together into a dark booth that smelled of cigarette smoke, Pine Sol, and stale semen.

New at sex, I was awkward and anxious and clumsy. But here was another person like me. I was allowed to touch another guy's body and it felt glorious. Hugging was amazing and the other sensations—well, I didn't know my body could feel so good. Sex felt like a type of grace that cared for the part of me I most despised.

But the experience was quickly over. The person left and I realized I now felt as bad as I had felt good. As I walked out of the store everything in my upbringing screamed that having gay sex was filthy, sinful, shameful, wicked, and disgusting. But I didn't just feel guilty about *doing* something bad, I felt the shame of feeling that my very *being* was bad.

That sense that such "badness" was really, truly, completely me, settled in with such force that I bent at the knees and laid down on the litter-strewn, urine-sprayed sidewalk outside the store.

I had been depressed and despairing before, and had even contemplated ending my life, but that night, as I lay on the sidewalk in front of an adult bookstore, the fact that the Mission Street pawn shops sold guns began to seem like a solution. I wondered if I would need a permit to buy one. Could they just check a driver's license? Would they have bullets for the gun?

Finally, I became aware of people walking out of their way to get around me, and I managed to get up, bypass the pawn shops, go home, and take a shower. As I stood in the warm water, naked and ashamed, I resolved that Dobson's advice hadn't worked. I had tried as hard as I could to be "normal." I had to tell someone, and I had to deal with being gay.

Good News

Now, over twenty-five years later, when I pass that place in my city, I am reminded of the poor choice I made that day, and I also remember the pain of growing up gay.

Now, as then, I wish that somehow, rather than ending up in the arms of that anonymous man, I could have found myself in the arms of the church. I wish the church had communicated to me that it could be trusted with my deepest secret, with my sense of alienation, with my self-loathing. I wish in the church I had found myself loved.

I've heard a phrase—sometimes mistakenly attributed to Saint Augustine—that rings true for me, "The church is a whore, but she's our mother." This book is my attempt to talk with mother church. Realizing I'm a part of mother church, I want us to do better by our children.

I sometimes understand the church as lying on that sidewalk. We're a mess. We've been fighting with each other and have done poorly by our gay and lesbian and transgendered children. The world sees us as an embarrassment and sidesteps us.

I don't think the solution to our problems is simply a matter of choosing the "right" position. Whether liberal (affirming) or conservative (traditional), we can all reflect on the debate about homosexuality and seek to faithfully incarnate Jesus rather than churning out a doctrinally "correct" position paper.

Let's get up off the sidewalk and give the church another shot. Better yet, by faith, let's invite God to raise us up. And maybe this time we'll look and act more like Jesus—which would be good news for us and for the whole world.

Questions for Discussion

1. Do you know anyone who identifies as LGBT? If so, how has your interaction with that person affected how you think about the topic of homosexuality?

2. Is there anything in your life that helps you resonate with the story related in this chapter?

3. How do you imagine the church could care for someone with the kind of history narrated in this chapter?

2

Hitting the Jackpot

"O poverty, source of all my riches.
Jesus give to me a heart that is trusting."

—Taizé chant

A British interviewer once said to the writer James Baldwin, "When you were starting out as a writer, you were black, impoverished, homosexual. You must have said to yourself 'Gee, how disadvantaged can I get?'" To which Baldwin responded, "Well no, I thought I hit the jackpot!"[1]

Growing up homosexual, I believed being gay was a liability that would make good people hate me if they knew the truth about me. I now realize that I hit at least one "winning number" in life's jackpot. Being gay helped me by forcing me to ask deeper questions of the world than I might have otherwise, and caused me to listen carefully to Jesus because I knew that I needed help.

After spending the summer in San Francisco, a summer filled with as many emotional ups and downs as the city has hills, I returned to college with the conviction that I needed to tell someone about my attraction to guys.

So I decided to tell my friend Thomas, who loved Old Testament theology, wrote love poems to God, and cared passionately for the oppressed. One night I gathered the courage to knock on Thomas's dorm room door and then asked him to take a walk with me. As we walked under the buzzing glow of street lights, I blurted out my feelings of attraction for guys. I soon ran out of words and scanned his face. Thomas furrowed his brow, but we walked on in

1. *James Baldwin.*

the wordless, blue buzz. Finally, breaking that tense moment, Thomas admitted that he, too, was gay.

I had seen graffiti on bathroom walls in the dorm saying things like, "Bob is a fag," but I had trouble believing that others at this Christian school had the same attractions, so Thomas's sexual orientation was a complete surprise to me. In retrospect I'd love to say I delighted in finding out that my friend was also gay—that we went on to support and encourage each other. But we both felt overwhelmed and ashamed of who we were. Our mutual revelations felt confusing, humiliating, and heavy.

A couple of weeks later I went to Thomas's house, and we ended up sitting on the couch together. I noticed beautiful flecks of yellow in his brown eyes. And then his eyes seem to grow bigger and I felt as though I was being enveloped by them and drowning in them. All at once I was infatuated, giddy and yearning and fused with my friend. For the first time, I felt in my body what all the movie kisses and love song lyrics are about.

As time went on and my feelings for him became evident, Thomas told me he was going to counseling and that I should consider it as well. I took his advice, hunted down the counseling center, and signed up.

A False Hope

It was a relief to talk to someone about the feelings and thoughts I had hidden for all of my life. Simply telling another human what went on in my head was helpful. The counselor did not run out of the room in horror, nor did she seem repulsed, revolted, or even surprised as I told her about my attraction to men. She helped me gain some perspective on my sexuality. Sure, I had a "problem," but other areas of my life like school and work were relatively okay.

My counselor listened well and also helped me listen to myself. But as I pressed her for a "fix it" solution, our sessions stalled. Toward the end of the semester, she recommended I attend a group called Desert Stream, a ministry focused on helping homosexuals find "healing."

As the next semester began I eagerly attended Desert Stream's orientation. After a talk about the "science" behind orientation change, or "reparative therapy," the presenter started a slide show featuring pictures of a handsome guy who picked up other guys at bars. As two Kodak projectors alternated slides, each dissolving into the next, the story unfolded of how he woke up one morning depressed and ashamed after a night of anonymous sex. He then repented, went to a lot of meetings, found a beautiful woman, and started a family. The last slide featured him with a wife and kids in front of a nice suburban house. As the soundtrack swelled, and as the last, soft-focus slide of the happy family faded to black, I felt like I had found the way to salvation. Again, I signed up.

I tried as hard as I could to repent of homosexuality. On Sundays, after church, I fasted and spent the day praying. I attended the weekly Desert Stream meeting. A long-haired, attractive man with a perm led us through earnest worship songs, a time of prayer ("If any phallic images are entering your mind, rebuke them in the name of Jesus!"), and a teaching time. We then divided into small groups. I did my homework and worked on issues of forgiveness, resisting pornography, and knowing myself to be loved. Those skills served me well. However, I was less successful at getting in touch with my inner manhood, forgiving my overbearing mom (she wasn't), and developing an attraction to women.

At the end of the year we were supposed to graduate. The implication was that I was now "repaired," but I knew I wasn't "fixed." And after getting to know many of the other thirty-five participants, I was fairly certain the others weren't "fixed" either.

Thomas didn't fare any better than I did, although he tried harder. At one point Thomas was going to counseling sessions five days a week. Eventually, sick of trying to "have more faith," sick of trying to "repent" for something he had never chosen in the first place, sick of stressing about it and loathing himself, Thomas gave up on Christianity.

Years later I met Steve, who became a good friend. Steve had gone through ten years of "reparative therapy." As part of the therapy he had "recovered memories" that his father had molested him. That caused huge damage to his relationship with his father, and eventually Steve realized his "memories" of abuse were false. Steve, too, left the faith.

Although I recognize these stories are anecdotes, and I've conducted no clinical trials, my sense is that "reparative therapy" creates more ex-Christians than it does ex-gays. I suspect that many of the "success" stories are people who were bisexual in the first place. Perhaps the therapy genuinely did work for a small percentage of people, and perhaps God did miracles for others, but holding out orientation change as a real option for most homosexuals is a false hope. The American Psychological Association has long been skeptical of such therapy. Recently, after reviewing eighty-three studies of "orientation change," it reaffirmed its position that true orientation change is rare and went on to note that reparative therapy can cause depression and even suicide.[2]

God sometimes answers our specific prayers, but we all know some prayers, even those said with great faith, aren't answered in precisely the way we desire. That doesn't mean we failed in prayer, or that God didn't answer.

2. *Report of the American Psychological Association.*

Living by faith might prompt us to look for ways God is at work, especially in ways we didn't expect. I believe sometimes God answers our specific petitions. But to preach that all Christians should expect a change of sexual orientation if they "just have enough faith" is cruel.

Losing Lottery Ticket

With my failure at orientation change, I began asking myself difficult questions. Had I not tried hard enough? How would I know if I had tried hard enough? If I fainted from fasting and prayer, would that be enough? My faith muscles seemed about worn out. At times I questioned faith itself. But I had been taught that Christianity is not a supernatural self-help scheme. Christianity means following Jesus in the way of the cross. That God hadn't changed me into a heterosexual wasn't necessarily evidence that Christianity is false.

I also took comfort in thoughts like Robert Farrar Capon's meditation in *The Astonished Heart:*

> He comes to us in the brokenness of our health, in the shipwreck of our family lives, in the loss of all possible peace of mind, even in the very thick of our sins. He saves us in our disasters, not from them. He emphatically does not promise to meet only the odd winner of the self-improvement lottery; he meets us all in our endless and inescapable losing.[3]

I briefly considered trying to marry a woman in spite of my orientation. I'd heard of some couples who got married even though one partner was a homosexual, and I didn't see anything wrong with this as long as there was full disclosure by the homosexual partner. But the prospect of lying in bed every night with someone whom I wasn't attracted to (emotionally or physically) seemed daunting to me. It also seemed unfair to whomever I might marry.

For awhile, I felt lost. But as I've already related, Jack challenged me to see my situation through the eyes of faith. And, as I adopted that lens, what seemed like a losing lottery ticket began to glimmer with possibility. I had to think hard about family and look to Jesus for answers. The answers, while difficult to realize, spoke of the gospel and a kingdom I had never imagined.

---

3. Capon, *Astonished Heart*, 15.

Questions for Discussion

1. Have you ever asked God to heal you of something? If God healed you, how do you relate to people who have prayed and yet have not received healing? If God didn't heal you, how do you think about that experience now?

2. To what extent is it helpful to think of the difficulties in your life as a curriculum? Are there any dangers in that?

3

The Bundle of Life

"The African would understand perfectly well what the Old Testament meant when it said 'man belongs to the bundle of life,' that he is not a solitary individual. He is linked backwards to the ancestors whom he reveres and forward with all the generations yet to be born. He believes in what H. Wheeler Robinson called, 'corporate personality.' Even today when you ask an African how he is, you usually in fact speak in the plural 'How are you?' and we will usually answer, 'We are well, we are here,' or the opposite; he will not be well because his grandmother is unwell, his vitality will be diminished in so far as one member of the family has reduced life force. The West suffers from an excessive individualism which makes man lonely in a crowd. Thoreau has aptly said of the population of modern cities, 'That millions are lonely together.'"

—Desmond Tutu

On the back of the book *Preparing for Adolescence,* I studied a picture of James Dobson with his wife, son, daughter, and a dog. It was similar to the pictures Desert Stream used in its slide presentations. Of all the advertising pictures that have worked on my soul, those reached me most profoundly.

I grew up living a terrific version of those pictures. My mother fixed us breakfast and dinner every day. On Wednesday night, family night, we would have a devotional together, a "family meeting," and then watch a TV show. Holidays were a delight—feasts filled with laughter, singing in four-part harmony, skits featuring my outrageous uncles, and often a trip to help build a

Habitat house or to sing at a local convalescent home. I loved my family and wanted one of my own.

Obviously I'm not the only one who wants this. Conservatives say they are trying to protect the traditional family and liberals say gays should have access to it.

The debate over same-sex relationships presents the church with a chance to ask the fundamental question: what is God's picture of family? What did Jesus teach about family?

Unless we ask these key questions and then let the emerging conflict guide us to appropriate answers, both sides will remain locked in argument.

Jesus' Family Values

Jesus does teach some "family values." Perhaps aware that his own father had contemplated "sending away" his mother, Jesus speaks against divorce in all three synoptic Gospels (Matt 5:31–32, 19:8–9; Mark 10:11; Luke 16:18). Jesus also criticizes the Pharisees and teachers of the law for devising traditions that deprived their parents of support owed to them (Matt 15:1–6). Jesus frequently cites the commandment to honor one's father and mother (Matt 15:4, 19:19; Mark 7:10, 10:19; Luke 18:20). And finally, Jesus welcomes children and affirms the importance of their nurture (Mark 9:37, 10:13–16; Luke 18:15–17).

What is startling is how often Jesus speaks against and disrupts family. Near the beginning of his ministry, Jesus calls the brothers James and John away from the family business of fishing. They follow Jesus, forsaking their father Zebedee in the boat with the hired hands (Mark 1:19–20). Jesus later tells a would-be-disciple who wants to bury his father to "let the dead bury their own dead" (Luke 9:60). On the question of who can be a disciple, Jesus says a disciple must "*hate* father and mother, wife and children, brothers and sisters" (Luke 14:26). When Jesus says he has not come to "bring peace, but a sword," he relates it to the family (Matt 10:34). "One's foes will be members of one's own household" (Matt 10:36).

Commentators and preachers often minimize the offense of these sayings, but given the importance of family within first-century culture, Jesus' words must have seemed *more offensive* in their original context. New Testament scholar N. T. Wright says, "In a peasant society, where familial relations provided one's basic identity, it [Jesus' teaching on family] was shocking in the extreme. . . . It cannot but have been devastating."[1]

---

1. Wright, *Jesus*, 278.

13

Why did Jesus say such inflammatory things about family? In all three synoptic Gospels, Jesus' mother and brothers come looking for him. When Jesus is told about this, rather than inviting them in, he looks at the crowd and declares, "My mother and my brothers are those who hear the word of God and do it" (Luke 8:21). With this offensive statement, Jesus was founding a new family around doing God's will. As Wright comments, "Jesus was proposing to treat his followers as a surrogate family. This had a substantial positive result: Jesus intended his followers to inherit all the closeness and mutual obligations that belonged with family membership in that close-knit, family-based society."[2]

While in college, I found extraordinary hope in these aspects of Jesus' teaching. Because I had always been on the outside of the in-crowd, I felt like Jesus was telling me, "you're already in." It was thrilling to think that as a believer, I was included in Jesus' family. I yearned for the relationships that Jesus describes in this new family of disciples.

In John 13, Jesus tells his disciples they are to love each other with the highest love, even to the point of laying down their lives for one another. Rather than celebrating the Passover with his family, as was the custom, Jesus celebrates with his disciples. During the meal, he washes their feet and instructs them to wash one another's feet. Then, before laying down his own life, he prays to the Father that this group would be united just as the family of Father, Son, and Spirit is united.

While I loved the challenge and idealism of Jesus' vision, it was painfully clear we weren't living this out at my Christian college. During my sophomore year I got sick with a high fever. My roommate disappeared and slept in another room because he was afraid of catching my illness. That night, delirious with fever, I wandered outside in my underwear, and—thinking I was fighting in Vietnam—made machine-gun noises as I attacked the dorm floodlights, convinced they were oncoming enemy helicopters.

As I recovered alone in my room, I was angry at my roommate for deserting me, though I knew that if he had been sick, I might have fled to another room as well. I knew that if we were going to be family to one another, we would need to stick with each other, even if it meant potential harm to ourselves. I began to wonder if Jesus really intended for us to act towards one another as though we were family. And I began to ask how the rest of the New Testament authors understood Jesus' teachings about family.

2. Ibid., 278.

Family in the New Testament

The idea of seeing fellow believers as first family is picked up by Paul and the other writers of the New Testament. In numerous passages, such as Acts 1:15, the gathered Christians are referred to as simply "the brothers." Here and elsewhere, the familial meaning of the Greek word *adelphoi* ("brothers") is sometimes obscured by our modern translations. The NRSV and NIV both often translate this as "the believers."[3] This term would be better translated as "brothers and sisters." In addition to using other language for family, the New Testament uses the word *adelphoi* in relation to Christians over a hundred times.

The only noun used more often than "brothers" in relation to Christians is the word "disciples." The use of this word is deceptive, because the vast majority of the time, "disciples" is used to specify the twelve. The word "saints" is used eighteen times; the word "believers" just three times. Christians are called followers of the "the Way" four times in Acts.

In the New Testament, the most common word for Christians in general is the family word *adelphoi. Brothers and sisters.* We tend to miss both the strength of that word and the challenge of it.

Joseph Hellerman, in his book *When the Church Was a Family,* points out that for first-century Jews, brother and sister relationships were often more important and stronger than spousal relationships. In a patriarchal culture, people gave primary loyalty to their family of origin rather than the new family formed by a husband and wife. A spouse was chosen by the parents for how the union would benefit the clan. Compatibility with the daughter or son was an afterthought. Romantic love was not an ideal, and sometimes a husband would have more than one wife.

On the other hand, sibling relationships were often the longest standing and commanded the deepest loyalty. This helps explain the crazy story of Dinah and her brothers in Genesis 34. After Dinah is raped, her brothers demonstrate their loyalty to her by not only killing her rapist, but all the men of the town. Stories about siblings—Cain and Abel, Joseph and his brothers, Esau and Jacob—fascinated the Jews because they spoke deeply to their own experience. For the Jews, sibling relationships were often the strongest family relationship, and thus the language of brotherhood spoke powerfully to them.

---

3. See also Acts 14:2, 15:1, 3, 7, 13, 22, 32, 33, 38, 40, 16:2, 17:6, 10, 14, 18:18, 27, 21:7, 17, 28:14, 15, Rom 1:13, 7:1, 8:12, 10:1, among others.

For those of us who see the marital relationship as primary, we should not miss the power of the New Testament call to be brothers and sisters to one another.[4]

Jesus taught us what this radical family relationship should look like by speaking of how we should treat "one another" (the single word *allelon* in Greek). We are to wash *one another's* feet and love *one another* as Jesus loved us (John 13:14, 34, 35; 15:12, 17).

"One another" language abounds in the rest of the New Testament. We are told to "outdo *one another* in showing honor," "become slaves to *one another*," "bear *one another's* burdens," and "lay down our lives for *one another*" (Rom 12:10, Gal 5:13, Gal 6:2, 1 John 3:16). Four times we are exhorted to "Greet *one another* with a holy kiss" (Rom 16:16, 1 Cor 16:20, 2 Cor 13:12, 1 Pet 5:14)—presumably something like greeting each other with an embrace, as we do in Western culture. Out of the 102 verses that are translated as "one another" by the NRSV, we are told to love each other twenty-three times (and that's not counting the kissing verses!).

Growing up gay, I struggled to think of the gospel as "good news." But as I studied the New Testament teaching on family, I began to think family might be possible for me. I came to understand the fellowship of the believers, when rightly practiced, ought to resemble a family.

As I continued my reading, I eventually came across Rodney Clapp's excellent book *Families at the Crossroads*. Clapp's work helped me grasp another crucial piece, namely that *our usual conception of the traditional family is neither traditional nor biblical.*

The Fiction of the Traditional Family

What we think of as the "traditional" family has only been "traditional" in the West for a couple hundred years. The pictures of family offered by Dobson and Desert Stream were not handed down directly from heaven. Sociologists refer to the "traditional family" as "nineteenth century bourgeois" because this type of family developed during the Industrial Revolution.

Before the existence of the "traditional family," people lived together in extended family groupings or clans. This began to change in the eighteenth century as more modern farming techniques led to higher crop yields and increasing unemployment in rural areas. Thousands of people migrated to

---

4. See Hellerman's excellent book *When the Church Was a Family*, especially pages 46–52.

the cities, seeking jobs in the burgeoning factories. The extended family was disrupted and a whole new model of family was developed.

The developing industrial machine demanded specialization and mobility. Extended family ties got in the way of moving human cogs to wherever the industrial machine needed a spare part. Family ties weakened, and eventually the idea of a "single family dwelling" became the norm. Thus far before the discovery of the atom, what we now call the "nuclear family," consisting of parents and children, was born.

Knowing myself to be gay, I wondered if I was doomed to be the negative electron, eternally circling the "nuclear family" but never really finding my place. When I realized that the "traditional family" was a modern phenomenon, I began to see the possibility that Jesus might be calling us to a different form of family altogether.

That family is probably not the traditional "biblical family," for as Clapp points out, the "traditional" Israelite family would have included between fifty and one hundred members. Grandparents, nieces, nephews, cousins and in-laws all lived near each other in a small village rather than a single family house.

At the center of their "traditional family" structure was the belief that Israel's hope was not in "heaven" but in its sons and daughters. Thus males were expected to be married by age twenty. There was no Hebrew word for "bachelor," and to be a single male was to be a sterile "dry tree"—a tragedy similar to being a barren woman. For Israelites, marrying and having kids was a sacred duty.

Yet Jesus challenged this view of the traditional family. For one thing, there would have been little place for him as a single person. Beyond that, Jesus wanted Israel to know that participation in God's people had more to do with faith than with proper blood lines. Jesus didn't merely revise the "traditional family" with a few tweaks here and there. He revolutionized family by defining it as those who do God's will.

If the "traditional family" as we know it is a recent development and Jesus challenged the much longer-standing "traditional family" of his day we ought to be open to how God might call us to reorder our family life. This might allow us to react less defensively and participate positively in thinking Christianly about family.

Yet ironically, as I tried to share with Christians on both the right and left how Jesus and the New Testament make the church "first family," I got the feeling I was spreading "bad" news. Marriage is difficult, and raising a family requires a lot of sacrifice. People need encouragement to hang in there, and anything that calls family into question can feel threatening.

I felt stuck. How could I both embrace Jesus' teaching and encourage people in their vocations as wives and husbands, fathers and mothers?

The Family Idol

Jack Bernard helped me think through this by handing me J. A. Walter's book *Sacred Cows: Exploring Contemporary Idolatry,* which suggests that family has become an idol.

Because I'd grown up convinced that family was undervalued and under attack, this claim seemed counterintuitive to me. But Walter argues that the family is falling apart precisely *because we expect too much of it.*

We expect too much of a spouse and so become disappointed and seek divorce. Romantic songs and movies train us to believe another person is going to provide salvation, meeting all of our social, emotional, and relational needs. Walter argues that there are fewer practical reasons for family today, and because our reasons for family are connected to ultimate meaning and fulfillment, we engage in idolatry.

Because I was sympathetic to Walter's critique of how we overvalue family, I worried I was living out my gay bias and betraying my tradition. Perhaps I had unconsciously allowed myself to be recruited into the "homosexual agenda" to destroy the family. But as I read Walter's history, I found his case compelling.

Walter recounts how family used to be a necessity to make life work. Economically, family meant a spouse and children worked together to help raise food or to work the family trade. A spouse helped create and raise children who were then expected to care for the parents as they aged. Socially, family gave people connections in the community as well as a sense of identity and belonging. Politically, the family name gave people rights to mutual protection and help in case of attack, famine, or disease.

But in our modern Western world, such a family structure is no longer a necessity for a person's survival. We usually leave the home and the family to conduct economic or social activities. We commute to work and shop at the mall or online. Social activities are more likely to take place at a restaurant, café, bar, or in cyberspace. This strips family of many of its functions, leaving it the task of emotional care. Family is not a necessary partnership in economic or social endeavors as much as it is the dispenser of affection and support.

To use Wendell Berry's phrase, the home is not a "communion of workmates," but a "love nest."[5] As Walter says, "It is in the family, modern people

5. Berry, *Art of the Commonplace*, 113.

believe, that meaning, love and warmth are to be found. This is most clearly manifested in the notion of romantic love in which exclusive love between two people is seen as the highest form of human relationship."[6]

While this may seem perfectly normal to us, it puts more pressure on the family than ever before. If marriage is not for economic, political, and social purposes, then what is it for? Blaine J. Fowers answers that we've come to see the marriage license as a "contract for happiness."[7] We expect our spouse to make us happy, and if he or she doesn't, the contract is broken. A similar logic extends to children. Western culture tends to sentimentalize children and teaches us to find our purpose and meaning in them. If the children don't manage to provide happiness and meaning, the temptation is to walk away from the family.

Walter's book helped me realize that questioning the idol we've made of family doesn't destabilize the family. Rather, this questioning is part of the very medicine the family needs to be restored to health.

Families need the support of God's larger family—a kinship of believers God is creating around the world called church. To provide that kinship, and to fulfill its own calling, the church needs to understand itself as a family. I will try to explain that vision in the following chapter.

Questions for Discussion

1. What is your reaction, both emotional and rational, to Jesus' difficult sayings about the family?

2. Are there ways you've seen high expectations for family produce resentment and disappointment? To what extent do you see the modern nuclear family as a potential idol?

6. Walter, *Sacred Cows*, 48.

7. Fowers, *Beyond the Myth*, 59.

4

The Kingdom Family

"Jesus' own life and teachings underscore that marriage and family now take a back seat to the universal proclamation of God's salvation and the formation of a new 'first family'—a world-wide kingdom-building company, in which membership depends not at all on bloodlines, but on faith in the Messiah.

—Mary Stewart Van Leeuwen

The idea that the church can function as a family might seem like a good, but mostly theoretical, idea. Yet I've seen it happen.

After finishing college, I traveled around Central America for nine months, trying to learn Spanish and understand the Latin American political situation as I sifted through the implications of being gay.

Toward the end of my trip, I found myself alone on a bus, winding through the hills above Tegucigalpa, Honduras. It was a cool night, and the darkness hid the daunting poverty as the lights of the slums sparkled like gems scattered across the rolling hills. After months of listening to music with tuba bass lines, I was glad for the US pop music on the radio. Above the driver, an LED cross blinked to the beat of the music next to a Playboy bunny sticker. I had spent a lot of time traveling alone. In my isolation, one desire became achingly plain. I wanted to be with a man. The desire was clear, fierce, and unrelenting. I felt a thrill of freedom race though my body. Nobody knew where I was. I had money in my pocket. I could do anything and go anywhere.

Pleasurable as that feeling was, I knew the excitement could quickly turn into a desolate loneliness. Though I longed to be with a male partner, I had been taught that longing was entirely corrupt. Yet everything was corrupt! I couldn't imagine a place, a way of being, a family, an economics, a politics in which any kind of life made sense. I was lost, with no place to be "found," no "home" to return to. That night, the path ahead seemed to diverge into two clear options. I could move to New York, cut off ties with my relatives and God and pursue a gay relationship. Or, I could sort out what it might mean to be both gay and Christian by moving back to San Francisco to the little church community that was being formed by my missionary friends.

I decided to take the road to San Francisco in order to give faith one last try.

So began my adventure at living in church community. Five young women from an InterVarsity chapter had helped start the community, which later came to be known as the Church of the Sojourners.[1] One night I sat down with them, and together we began looking through a pile of old yearbooks. As they reminisced, they pointed out the good-looking guys and I chimed in with my opinions. For the first time, I could be honest about my sexual thoughts, and they weren't followed by my inner retort, "Tim, you are so sick." For the first time, talking about sex seemed normal and connecting and even joyful. As we sat there talking and laughing I felt like I had found sisters.

Finding Family

They certainly acted like my sisters, making fun of my amateur cooking, shooting me withering looks when I greeted them cheerily in the early morning. They taught me to like good coffee and helped me grow out of being oblivious to what needed doing. One of the women in particular, Debbie, jumped in my corner like a trainer caring for a beleaguered boxer. She wrote me notes of encouragement, listened to me rant late into the night, and hugged me in a way that said, "I'm for you, keep going."

I had long talks with the older members, especially Jack, John, and Steve. I was glad to have wise elders to talk with, a welcome change from the generational ghetto of college. We ate dinners together, vacationed together, read books together, argued together, competed for bathroom time, and cleaned up after John's incontinent dog.

1. We are often confused with *Sojourners* magazine, which is based in Washington, D.C.

As good as life together was, we began to wonder, "Is this just a phase? An idealism that will pass?" We began to think about committing to each other in more costly, long-term ways. We'd been impressed by Jesus' last words to the disciples right before he went to the cross when he says, "I give you a new commandment, that you love one another. Just as I have loved you, you also should love one another" (John 13:34). I had realized that the phrase, "as I have loved you," meant the cross, and I imagined heroic scenarios in which I would jump into a river to save a drowning friend at the risk of my own life.

But there, living within this extended family, I noticed the placement of this verse, shortly after Jesus washes the disciples' feet. Maybe loving as Jesus loved isn't in spectacular acts such as hanging on a cross, but in serving one another by washing the pile of dishes in the sink and cleaning the toilet. Yes, Jesus asks for radical self-sacrifice, but he often expresses this in small things. Perhaps in the daily tasks of living with one another, bearing with one another over the long haul.

John Alexander, our pastor, frequently pointed out the verse in John, in which Jesus prays, "The glory that you have given me I have given them, so that they may be one, as we are one" (17:22). We are not only asked to love one another as Christ loved, but we are also asked to be one with each other as the Trinity is one!

Together, we began to think about the implications of this unity. If one of us moved away for the sake of more money, or a more prestigious job, what did that mean about our commitment to love one another? Were those relationships disposable? The expressive individualism of our culture told us our highest duty was to ourselves. But what did it mean to take Paul's words in his letter to the Philippians seriously when he exhorts, "Look not to your own interests but to the interests of others"? (Phil. 2:4).

Some of the members of our community decided to commit to each other until "we discern together God has called me elsewhere." Jack was asked by the mission agency he worked for to relocate from San Francisco to Colorado Springs. As regional director for a missionary agency, he joked that his job was to drive around and visit his friends. Even though Jack loved his job, he decided to quit rather than move, and take a poorly paid teacher's aide job in a local school so that he could continue living with the rest of us.

One of the five women, Laura, knew that choosing to live in a poor, urban area with others would alienate her closely knit family. After much agonizing, Laura decided she needed to live out the life she thought would please God, even if it didn't please her family.[2] The five young, single women living in our

---

2. For years, Laura's mom refused to visit the house. Happily, that has now changed.

Christian "commune" in San Francisco knew such a lifestyle didn't promise much in the way of marriage prospects.[3] Three of them chose to stay anyway.

In *The Brothers Karamazov*, Dostoyevsky writes:

> Everywhere in these days people have, in their mockery, ceased to understand that true security is to be found in social solidarity rather than in isolated individual effort. But this terrible individualism must inevitably have an end, and all will suddenly understand how unnaturally they have separated themselves from one another. It will be the spirit of the time, and people will marvel that they have sat so long in darkness without seeing the light.[4]

Being gay, I had felt that "social solidarity" and "family" were impossible for me. Yet with my brothers and sisters in the Church of the Sojourners, I felt like I was suddenly coming to the surface and encountering light after years of living in an underground cave. I was living in a New Testament family, in which I was loved, and in which others needed my love.

Coming Home

My evangelical tradition had taught me that, being gay, I would need to remain single. As I grieved not having my own family, I struggled to understand Jesus' teaching on family, which yielded some surprising insights.

Ironically, the traditional and affirming churches are mirror images of each other, with the traditional side worrying that same-sex marriages will erode the "traditional family," and the affirming side demanding that gays and lesbians have access to the "traditional family." Both sides are assuming our culture's vision of family rather than inviting the conflict to help us think about Jesus' kingdom vision of family.

If we can agree to trust that the conflict over homosexuality is not a battle to be won, but rather an opportunity to grow, then our deepest conceptions—which are often products of our culture—might be reformed by the Christian vision. If we invite God to shape our ideas about family, we might discover what it means to be a church. And, as I explore in the next chapters, this journey might also call us to rethink the ethics of our economics and politics as well.

On the far side of this struggle, we might come "home" to a surprising unity. As with any large family, Christians will never agree about everything. But at least our conflicts might assume the loving tenor of a couple fighting *for*

3. All three eventually got married. For two, it meant waiting to marry until they were in their thirties.

4. Dostoyevsky, *The Brothers Karamazov*, 276.

a good marriage, rather than the ugly, divisive debates of a couple headed for divorce.

Questions for Discussion

1. Are you part of a church that acts as family to each other?

2. How might you grow in relating to each other as brothers and sisters?

Relating a siblings means no giving up. Finding resolution and understanding. Forgiveness and acceptance.

5

It's the Economy, Stupid!

"Consumerism says that the individual consumer is the center of meaning and everything that comes before each one of us—including our relationships—is an object of exchange that can ultimately be directed toward our satisfaction."

—Kurt Armstrong

As I was thinking about family during my college years in the mid-1980s, the culture wars were heating up. Years earlier, pop singer Anita Bryant had helped ignite the culture wars by organizing the coalition "Save Our Children," making statements such as, "As a mother, I know that homosexuals cannot biologically reproduce children; therefore, they must recruit our children."[1] Conservative evangelical organizations were raising money for "pro-family" efforts against the "homosexual agenda." They made troubling statements about the family being "under attack."

As I pondered Jesus' harsh statements about family, I came to understand them as warnings against making the family an idol that gets in the way of joining God's family. Family in itself is a beautiful and God-given gift, which is why it is a tempting idol. I had no intention to harm the family. Rather, the very source of my pain was my exclusion from family.

Moreover, as far as I could tell, most gays and lesbians thought marriage and family were something sacred and important, which is why they were fighting so hard for the right to get married. So it was difficult for me to believe

1. "Anita Bryant," lines 33–35.

25

the charge by conservative Christians that homosexuals were trying to tear apart marriage and family.

But I had to agree that families were struggling. The key question was: Why? This question is as relevant today as it was in the mid-1980s. If homosexuals aren't the cause of the family's troubles, why are families struggling?

As I reflect on this question, it seems that divorce and changing sexual ethics are symptoms rather than causes of the struggle. Put more concretely, conservative, evangelical, "pro-family" organizations have been fighting the wrong enemy. The family was never under attack by homosexuals, but by consumer capitalism. Consumer capitalism undermines the family by:

1. Giving us less incentive to create strong families;

2. Promoting mobility, which weakens support for the family;

3. Training us to see ourselves as consumers and other people as products.

As we understand the real cause of the family's struggles we'll realize that there is no group of convenient scapegoats. Parents and children, single, married and divorced, conservative and liberal, gay and straight, we are all in this fight together.

Money: More Reliable than Relatives

In pre-industrial times, most families relied on children for income and labor. Children helped in the fields or worked in the family trade. To adults, children were a financial asset and also served as a security net in one's old age. Because of this, people had a strong incentive to nurture the male-female marriage bond and protect the marriage covenant. Often, people's very survival—their ability to get enough food—depended on the strength of their family.

How different life is today! The US Federal government estimates that middle-class families will spend an average of $235,000 to raise a child for seventeen years.[2] Most children, rather than expecting to support their parents financially in their old age, expect the parents to be self-sufficient and give them an inheritance. The economic motivation to have a strong family has collapsed.

Our sense of security resides less in our children and extended family ties. Instead, our economy trains us to see security as having a lot of money. Having money means that if we get divorced, or if the kids do something crazy like take low-paying teacher jobs, the adult individual still has the basics of shelter and food covered. With this change comes the subtle temptation to

2. Cohn, "Cost of Raising."

invest more in our jobs than in relationships. Surely, we tell ourselves—for our most basic needs of food, shelter, and safety—money in the bank is more reliable than relatives.

Our Western economic system has created a loss of biblical values such as faithfulness, perseverance, selflessness, and the willingness to undergo difficulty for the sake of others. To state it simply, we don't have as much need for these values today, because our economy has made it possible to "go it alone" and shed the difficulty of relating to and relying on others.

The Cost of Mobility

In *Sacred Cows: Exploring Contemporary Idolatry,* Walter explains how our economy's demand for mobility also undermines families. The industrial machine draws people to where it most needs them by offering jobs or higher salaries in those places. When people move long distances, they sever ties with their extended family of grandparents, uncles, aunts, and cousins. The result is decreased support from family, which puts more stress on an individual, or a marriage relationship, than ever before.

Because I moved a lot as a missionary kid, attending eighteen different schools by the time I started college, I experienced how mobility made it difficult to keep good relationships with family and friends.

Even though I studied at the same college for four years (an increasingly rare experience), I was surprised to discover how transitory the relationships were. In my sophomore year, my best friend moved to attend a less expensive school. During my junior year, my best friend moved back to Canada. I spent the second semester of my junior year in Washington D.C., where I made an entirely new set of friends. When I returned from D.C., I knew my friends and I would be scattering in nine months.

Having experienced relationships as short-lived until my early twenties, I desperately yearned for at least one person who would go with me wherever life took me.

Today I live in California where families move an average of every three years. As married couples chase economic opportunities presented by further education, better jobs, or cheaper and better houses, they hardly have time to make friends in the neighborhood, at church, or even at work before they move again. People come, and people go. Although the faces change, these individuals share similar traits: their marriages absorb the stresses of these moves, and they expect the marriage relationship to be the place where the majority of their relational, emotional, and social needs are met.

It is the unusual relationship that can support all these relational expectations. A spouse is demanding an awful lot to ask one other person to fill the shoes of missing friends, relatives, and co-workers. So married people file for divorce, or seek sex outside the marriage, or simply seethe with poisonous resentment that their spouse isn't meeting all their needs.

This stress on the family isn't the fault of the members of the conservative, nuclear family down the street who fail to live up to their "pro-family" ideals. Nor is it the fault of the lesbians next door who have made promises to love each other for a lifetime. This stress is the fault of our modern economy, and it's time we start telling the truth about that.

I'm a Consumer and You Are a Product

Our economy does more, however, than remove our incentives to invest in strong families or scatter us to distant jobs that separate us from our loved ones. Our modern consumer capitalist society reaches into our hearts and mangles how we think of ourselves and others.

Our economy deforms our hearts through the thousands of advertisements it throws at us every day. The market research firm of Yankelovich claims that people living in cities have gone from seeing around two thousand ads a day thirty years ago to seeing roughly five thousand ads each day now.[3] These ads imply the constant message, "You are deficient." The collective message that these advertisers send is, "Your clothes are dirty and out of fashion. Your hair isn't sexy, silky, or shiny enough. Your car is slow. Your chest is too small and your tummy is too large. Your teeth are yellow and your complexion needs work. You're not attractive enough. You're stressed, and disconnected. You're missing out!"

Every ad tells the same story. You have a need, and our product or service can fill it. Told this story thousands of times a day, the sheer repetition and genius of the ads (thought up by some of the best minds of our time) win us to their logic. We begin to believe we are mostly a bundle of needs that can be relieved with the right products and services.

President Herbert Hoover, trying to stimulate the economy in the midst of the Great Depression, told Americans to think of themselves as "happiness machines." The idea was that, like machines, we need the raw materials of goods and services; as we consume them, we will produce happiness for ourselves and others.

3. Story, "Anywhere the Eye," para 7.

It is interesting that on social media sites such as Facebook, we often convey our identities in terms of what we consume. Rather than primarily listing character traits and commitments as showing who we are, we list the movies, music, books, TV shows, and sports programming we consume.

Rodney Clapp, in his excellent article "Why the Devil Takes Visa," summarizes the kind of people our economic system produces:

> The consumer is schooled in insatiability. He or she is never to be satisfied—at least, not for long. The consumer is tutored that people basically consist of unmet needs that can be appeased by commodified goods and experiences. Accordingly, the consumer should think first and foremost of himself or herself and meeting his or her felt needs. The consumer is taught to value above all else freedom, freedom defined as a vast array of choices.[4]

The problem with this way of thinking is that we end up applying this logic to our relationships, and this logic is undermining the family.

When I bought my second cell phone, I used an online "screener" website. This website allowed me to select the carrier I wanted, the price I was willing to pay, the type of monthly plan I wanted, the style of phone, and the features I wanted on my phone. When I was done, the web site presented me with a variety of phones to choose from. I ordered one, knowing that if I didn't like it, I could return it within thirty days and try another.

Without doubt, this website provides a terrific method for ordering a phone and a service plan. But how different, essentially, is an online dating service? Users of an online dating service look for a mate by inputting the age, gender, religion, educational background, and interests of the kind of human they want to marry. Then they click through a few confirmation screens and arrange a date.

And sometimes it works.

But are we also buying into the expectations we have for online business transactions? If I don't like the person I ordered, can I return him or her? And if I find a better, newer model in a couple of years, can I return the outmoded one? What if my mate is defective? Sexually incompatible? Depressed? Do I get a one- or two-year warranty?

As I contemplate our consumer capitalist culture, I am disturbed by its similarities to the Babylon described in Revelation. In Revelation 18, the people of God are exhorted to come out of Babylon, a city described as having "glorified herself and lived luxuriously" (Rev 18:7). As God's judgment is executed on the city, the merchants lament that no one buys, "gold, silver,

---

4. Clapp, "Why the Devil," 28.

jewels and pearls, fine linen, purple, silk and scarlet, all kinds of scented wood, all articles of ivory, all articles of costly wood, bronze, iron, and marble, cinnamon, spice, incense, myrrh, frankincense, wine, olive oil, choice flour and wheat" (Rev 18:12–13).

As impressive as that list must have seemed in the ancient world, it hardly begins to imagine the modern-day mall, let alone the infinite choices available through Internet shopping. Then the passage takes a chilling turn, speaking of how the merchants lament that no one buys "cattle and sheep, horses and chariots, slaves—and human lives" (Rev 18:13).

The logic of the market ends up extending beyond products to people. Capitalism trains us to think of other people as designed to fill our emotional and psychological needs. We "network" and thus think of other people as business and social assets. We grow dissatisfied with friends and relations, thinking that if we just could exercise our freedom and make better "shopping" choices in regard to people, happiness will be ours.

Wendell Berry's character Jayber Crow makes a telling observation about this mentality of discontent:

> Theoretically, there is always a better place for a person to live, better work to do, a better spouse to wed, better friends to have. But then this person must meet herself coming back: theoretically, there always is a better inhabitant of this place, a better member of this community, a better worker, spouse, and friend than she is. This surely describes one of the circles of Hell, and who hasn't traveled around it a time or two?[5]

It is one thing to travel those circles of Hell a time or two, but our economic system is pushing us to do daily laps of discontent and dissatisfaction. Consumer capitalism shapes our desire to "trade up" in relation to spouses and friends, to "test drive" others before marriage, to relate to others as "friends with benefits."

Focusing on the Family of God

The conflict around homosexuality has caused the church to "focus on the family" and what ails it. Yet rather than focusing on how we can work together to become the family of God in the midst of a destructive culture, we are locked in debilitating cycles of blame and debate.

The Christian right has blamed the "homosexual agenda" as the cause of the family's woes. Though Jesus warns more about the dangers of money than

5. Berry, *Jayber Crow*, 210.

anything else, religious conservatives have ignored these teachings and seized instead a handful of biblical verses—none uttered by Jesus—to condemn homosexuality and blame homosexuals for the devaluation of marriage. Thus they locate evil as "out there." But rather than scapegoating gays and lesbians, the church needs to admit its complicity with capitalism and how our modern consumer culture is destroying the family.

On the religious left, the church has bought into a consumerist transaction model of marriage, where a marriage's function is to meet each partner's felt needs. Each partner is encouraged to see the spouse as a kind of service provider, who is prompted to meet the other's needs through carefully honed communication skills. In marriages of this variety, if one partner doesn't feel happy and satisfied, the marital "contract" is broken.

This fragile view of marriage is also shaped by consumer capitalism, rather than the teachings of Christ. By ignoring the covenantal nature of the Christian faith and how that extends to human relationships in marriage, this model has made liberal sexual ethics justifiably suspect to conservative Christians.

If we are going to live as salt, light, and leaven amidst our modern consumer culture, we will need to work together to identify the real threats to family and think about how we might, as the family of God, become part of the cure.

As Christians, how might we guard against the logic of the market so that it doesn't distort our relationships with family and friends? How might we be a light to a culture that cheapens marriage and friendship?

Questions for Discussion

1. How would you describe the complex relationship between economics and human relationships to someone in your church or family?

2. How has consumer capitalism formed your thinking? Has that thinking distorted and damaged your relationships? How?

3. How would you engage this conversation with someone with whom you disagree?

6

Gospel Economics

"In the Far East there is a traditional image of the difference between heaven and hell. In hell, the ancients said, people have chopsticks one yard long so they cannot possibly reach their mouths. In heaven, the chopsticks are also one yard long—but, in heaven, the people feed one another."

—Joan Chittister

All Things in Common

While it is hardly possible to cut ourselves off from the modern economy, the church needs to consider how to resist the destructive consumer mindset and form an alternative economic culture that embraces people as more than merchandise.

The early church lived such an alternative economic culture where Christians shared "all things in common" (Acts 2:32, 44–45). At Sojourners, we've tried to grapple with the witness of the early church to find modern expressions of gospel that challenge our deformed thinking. As we have experimented with economics inspired by the early church, we have discovered the gift of relating to others as people rather than products.

In the early years of our church community, we talked about how to make living as family to one another real. We realized families share space, time, and money—but money seemed like a particularly sensitive topic. We discussed how we knew more about our co-workers' sexual lives than their financial lives. Some of us had piles of debt and others stashes of stocks. Some of us reveled in being generous, while others relished simple living. As we shared about our financial lives, we began to realize that as a culture, we had come to believe that money was central to our security and dictated our peace and happiness. Talking with others about our relationship to money meant having those false ideas challenged.

An Openhanded Culture

We realized we needed a whole new economic culture, one that encouraged work, but not for the sake of money and status. A culture that encouraged generosity, but not through grandiose store-bought gifts. A culture that encouraged simplicity, but not stinginess.

At one point a community member asked us to "Clench your fist hard and hold it tight for thirty seconds. Look at the white-knuckles it creates. Now . . . open your fist and notice how good that feels." We stared at our relaxed, open palms and wondered how to create a culture of openhandedness. How to receive with gratitude all God gives us and, with faith, give all God asks of us.

Eventually, we made some concrete decisions. We decided that each of us would have the same modest standard of living. We each paid rent, food, and transportation and then kept $275 as discretionary spending.[1] This meant one of our members, a developmentally delayed Salvadoran woman with a low-wage, part-time job, had the same amount of spending money as our successful computer programmer. Any money we earned beyond the agreed upon limit was pooled. We agreed we would decide together how to spend that money.

Because we pooled our money, we were able to buy houses in San Francisco, give away buckets of bills to needy people around the world, support church community staff, and throw the occasional lavish party.

We realized that participation in this different economy meant we were putting most of our money and time into kingdom investments. While we encouraged modest savings, above all we worked to buy the pearl of great price. That has helped us count on God's way and people for our continued well-being—even as we age—rather than on money.

---

1. The system was and is a little more complex than that. Certain other expenses, such as health expenses, were (and are) considered non-discretionary. We still haven't figured out exactly how to think about savings and retirement. And we've increased the monthly discretionary spending to $335.

The Gift of Stability

As I mentioned in the previous chapter, consumer capitalism subtly encourages us to devalue relationships by encouraging us to move for our jobs.

At the Church of the Sojourners, because of our financial commitment to one another, no one needs to move from financial necessity. If you are part of our church, your financial needs are taken care of as long as you are making an effort to find work. This kind of security has occasionally allowed members to witness to others the abundance of God's kingdom.

One of our members, Edith, was working at a plumbing supply company that was struggling financially and needed to lay off an office worker. It became clear that either Edith or another woman would be laid off. Edith volunteered to be laid off because she knew her church community would take care of her. Just a week after Edith quit work, we received a call from an acquaintance asking if we knew of anyone who could do office work at a plumbing supply company! It felt like a clear act of God's provision.

In trying to act like family to one another, we commit to not moving away unless "we discern together that God is calling me elsewhere." In our discernment, we don't see moving for the sake of a job with higher pay or prestige as kingdom values. If a person or family is feeling a strong calling to do kingdom work elsewhere, we tend to bless that. Otherwise, for the sake of relationships, we tend toward the wisdom of Abba Anthony, "In whatever place you live, do not easily leave it."[2]

Our economy teaches us to be discontent, and often we think a change of setting will make us happy. But more and more, we're experiencing the wisdom of the Twelve-Step slogan: "If the grass is greener on the other side of the fence, it is probably because your neighbor stays home and waters it."

As Jonathan Wilson-Hartgrove says in his book *The Wisdom of Stability*, "the practice of stability is the means by which God's house becomes our home."[3] Even if the members of our church are not our natural affinity group (a testament that it is God bringing us together rather than our own taste in friends), as we go through the difficulties and joys of life together, we become veterans of a common history and find ourselves bound together as brothers and sisters. These people become family. God's house becomes home.

The practice of stability helps us reaffirm, again and again, that we value people over the false bliss promised to us by more wealth and status. Capitalism teaches us dissatisfaction with what we have and promises that happiness will be ours if we buy a new product. Thus we are tempted to trade in spouses

2. Wilson-Hartgrove, *Wisdom of Stability*, 35.

3. Ibid., 17.

and friends, believing other people will make us happier. But by committing to stay where we are, in the relationships we've been given, we are forced to grow and tend the relationships around us. This is a concrete way of resisting the logic of the market.

Abundantly Satisfied

As I contend in the previous chapter, one of the most devious and dangerous aspects of a consumer economy is that it teaches us to see ourselves as bundles of unmet needs—needs that must be satisfied by consuming products, services, and people.

The temptation is similar to the temptation Adam and Eve faced. God had provided abundantly, yet the serpent convinced them that God was holding out on them. Rather than having faith in God, they believed the serpent's lie that somehow the fruit from the tree in the middle of the garden would provide them with wisdom they needed.

Paul's letter to the church at Ephesus focuses on how abundantly God has provided for each of us. We've been given "every spiritual blessing in the heavenly places," "his glorious grace that he freely bestowed on us in the Beloved," as well as "redemption through his blood, the forgiveness of our trespasses according to the riches of his grace," to say nothing of the "the riches of his glorious inheritance among the saints," alongside "the immeasurable greatness of his power for us who believe," and perhaps most importantly "the love of Christ that surpasses knowledge" (Eph 1:3, 6, 7, 18, 19, 3:19).

This list is so abundant, yet even with all these blessings, we go through life thinking that what we really need is a newer handheld gadget, an updated kitchen, or a faster car. To say nothing of thinking we need new and improved people—a different spouse, different children, different friends.

The challenge, then, is to have faith that God isn't holding out on us, but is giving us enough. Faith that God can work to make us into the people God wants us to be, even in the midst of our current relationships. Faith that God is good and is at work for the good.

Given over to God

Living with the spending limit we created at the Church of the Sojourners made me think hard about what I desired. Would my life really be better if I ate out more? Would I be more content if I could ski more? Jack Bernard kept reminding us that as followers of Jesus, what we really want is to be holy. He clarified that "holy" doesn't mean sinless, but rather "completely given over to God," a yearning in our hearts that usually goes unanswered.

Jack told us that historically some people aspired to be saints. In our day, saying you want to be a saint seems prideful. But the word "saint" is just another translation of "holy." When we turn away from the desire to be holy, to become a saint, we are saying, "God, you can have most of me, but I think I'll do better if I keep this certain part of life to run myself."

I realized I wanted to be a saint. More than anything I wanted to *get*, I wanted to *give* myself completely to God. I began to wonder about this logic in other parts of my life. Was it possible that even more than wanting to get love, I wanted to give love? That even more than wanting to get thanked, I wanted to give thanks? That even more than wanting to be esteemed, I wanted to esteem others?

What if I were to live that way? What if we were all to live that way? What if rather than believing the message of our consumer economy—that we are a bundle of unmet needs—we were to believe that we're gifted by God? When we believe that God has given us enough, we can then generously love, thank, esteem, give, serve, and help others. Imagine the abundance of a people living that way! In such an economy, most of our real needs would be taken care of.

We tried to come up with small ways to live into such an economy at Sojourners. It made me smile to think that, like the Christians in Acts, everything we owned "was held in common." Well, not everything . . . toothbrushes and quite a few other things were definitely private property. Nonetheless, it could be said of us, "There was not a needy person among them" (Acts 4:32b and 4:34a). And by living this way, I was receiving the fullness of Jesus' promise that those who followed him would receive "houses, brothers and sisters, mothers and children, and fields" (Mark 10:30b).

A different economic reality—a truly abundant life—was being made real among us.

Using Money to Love People—Not the Other Way Around

In retrospect, I've come to discover that a different economic vision not only helped the members of our community relate better to money and property, but also to our families and friends.

Our attempts to resist the logic of consumer capitalism aren't perfect. We are simply a small group of people attempting to "love people and use money, and not the other way around."[4]

But when we limit our spending, we remember we are provided for by God, rather than through consumer goods and services. This way of dependence on God helps us remember that spouses and friends are not products to be used and then returned to the store when they no longer make us happy, but rather gifts given by God so we might learn to love faithfully.

The logic of the consumer capitalist market extends beyond the mall to our homes and relationships, including our intimate sexual relations. Thus as we have lived towards a gospel way of thinking about money and people, our community's thinking about sex has also become more healthy.

Because we are not as tempted to see others as objects, we are better able to commit to lifetime relationships. Because we do not seek to fulfill our desires through consumer goods and services, or even other human beings, we are freed from idolatry to trust the infinite God of the universe to fulfill our needs. In this way, our church community has become a healthy stream that has enabled us as followers of Christ to "swim" a healthier sexual ethic. Without water, or in culturally toxic water, swimming such a healthy sexuality is next to impossible.

As followers of Christ, we need to stop blaming homosexuality for the destruction of family and marriage in our culture. Instead, we need to repent for the ways we buy into the logic of the market—which poses the most potent threat to the family—and in so doing, seek to heal the church, the broken family of God.

Questions for Discussion

1. How can you imagine doing economics differently in the context of your church? How can you help members of your church think more Christianly, so that they can "love people and use money, and not the other way around"?

2. Gandhi used the language of "experiments in truth" in relation to the different practices he adopted. Why might that kind of attitude be helpful in thinking about the adoption of different economic practices?

4. My parents repeated this phrase to me over and over.

7

Sacrificial Power

"While all the versions of the kingdom of the world acquire and exercise power over others, the kingdom of God, incarnated and modeled in the person of Jesus Christ, advances only by exercising power under others. It expands by manifesting the power of self-sacrificial, Calvary-like love."

—Pastor Gregory Boyd

Costly Righteousness

Although I was quite young when I lived as a missionary kid in Uganda, I remember the fear of living under the dictator Idi Amin.

Amin had ordered all guns to be taken away from the police so that his army would have absolute power. I remember when a gang of thieves tried to bash down our front gate with a bag of rocks and only moved on when our watchdog charged the fence. I remember finding my father's gun under his dresser—a gun held in reserve in case the front gate, the guard dog, the night watchman, and the four large padlocks on the front security door should fail. I remember the day Amin's agents came to our house and deported us, after confiscating our house, our car, and anything else we couldn't fit in our suitcases.

I began developing a fantasy life in which I was commander of the US Army, an army that would mow down all the bad guys. I was eight years old when we moved back to the United States, and I learned the president was the commander-in-chief of the armed forces. I promptly decided that was the job for me. Being bullied in elementary school and junior high, I responded by developing an elaborate fantasy life in which I was super-powerful.

When I started high school, I began to pursue that fantasy through a socially acceptable mode of wielding power: politics. I got involved in student government and daydreamed about becoming a congressman. A favorite uncle took me to a pro-life conference sponsored by Francis Schaffer and Surgeon General C. Everett Koop. After the conference, I put together a pro-life slide show with pictures of both healthy and aborted fetuses. I showed it at my church and to a couple of classes at my public high school.

While I thought I was right about abortion being wrong, I began to question my motivation. I was a closeted, gay virgin. I felt tremendous guilt about my own sexual thoughts and wanted a way to feel okay about myself. Campaigning against abortion made me feel righteous at no cost to myself.

Perhaps something similar is happening in the national debate over same-sex marriage. When conservative Christians crusade against homosexual rights, they are able to feel smugly self-righteous without paying any personal cost. As Christian influence within the culture wanes and sexual mores change, Christian rates of divorce,[1] and pornography use[2] are about equal to those of non-Christians.

Some years ago, for example, here in California, the religious right sponsored Proposition 8, which made same-sex marriage illegal in the state. Religious proponents of the measure said they did it in order to defend the institution of marriage. Because most of them, if not all of them, were heterosexual, Proposition 8 had little cost to them personally.

Yet if the religious right had wanted to promote a "biblical view" of marriage, they could have campaigned for stricter divorce laws. After all, Jesus himself said that people shouldn't divorce except in cases of adultery (Matt 5:32, Mark 10:11, Luke 16:18). He didn't say anything at all about homosexuality. But the conservative Christian proposition was aimed at a small group of gays and lesbians who had to bear the cost of their moral vision.

At the same time, Christians on the left are seeking to make their moral vision the law of the land. Non-discrimination clauses concerning sexual orientation may jeopardize federal and state funding for conservative Christian colleges and service organizations. As the country becomes more tolerant of homosexuality, the left may make the religious right pay dearly for its ethic.

The debate about homosexuality raises key questions that affect all of us: How are we to think about politics and power as Christians? How are we to

---

1. "New Marriage," Barna Group.
2. "Porn & Pancakes," CNN.com.

engage power and politics, particularly in relation to those who disagree with us?

Power Politics

In order to pursue my interest in politics, during my junior year of college I participated in the American Studies Program in Washington D.C. sponsored by the Christian College Coalition.

Having landed a semester-long internship working for a Christian congressman, I answered the endlessly ringing phones or acted as receptionist for the constant stream of people meeting with the congressman. But my main job was to answer the mail. For popular issues, we sent out form letters that had been written by the senior legislative aides. But sometimes, people wrote letters for which we had no formulated response. I would research the issue and then write a letter according to the office boilerplate.

The first paragraph always noted the constituent's concerns and underlined their importance. The second paragraph would qualify the previous paragraphs and raise concerns from the other side to allow the congressman some wiggle room in how he voted. The final paragraph would note the status of any bills involved, thank the person for writing, and assure the person that the congressman would "take your concerns into account as he votes on this issue."

I would then take the letter to the signature machine, insert a blue felt-tip pen into its writing arm, and watch with fascination as the machine penned a perfect replica of the congressman's signature on the letter. And off the letter went.

The thing that disturbed me was *there was no mechanism to communicate to the congressman what the incoming letters said.* On some important issues, we would collect statistics on the number of calls and letters "for" or "against," but this was mostly to justify the positions that the congressman already held.

Growing up I'd been told to vote—and if I really wanted to change things to "write to Congress." I began to see that real power lay not so much with the average concerned citizen who took the trouble to write Congress, but with the endless stream of lobbyists and Washington power brokers who paraded in and out of our office.

Kingdom Politics

I had to wonder, is that how God is transforming the world for the good? As I thought about access to power and the use of power, one of my professors at the American Studies Program asked a question that has continued to haunt me: "Isn't it odd to legislate that non-Christians live as if Jesus is Lord, when Christians don't live as if Jesus is Lord?"

The same professor had us read a book that functioned like a 9.0 earthquake in my political thinking: Anabaptist theologian John Howard Yoder's *The Politics of Jesus*, which makes the case that Jesus had a political agenda.

Growing up I'd been taught Jesus wanted to be Lord of our individual lives and the gospel had nothing to do with politics. The gospel centered on the question: "Have you asked Jesus Christ into your heart as your personal Savior?" I began to realize that Jesus' gospel was, "Repent for the Kingdom of God is near"—and "kingdom" is an exceedingly political word.

Jesus did not come to force everyone to live God's way. He didn't lead marches on Rome or use angel armies to set himself up as Emperor. Rather, he taught his disciples to live a new ethic, a new politics, a new way of exercising power toward each other as a light to the world.

Given this new lens, I began to notice all kinds of political verses I had previously not noticed. For instance, in Mark 10:42–44, Jesus says to his disciples: "You know that among the Gentiles those whom they recognize as their rulers lord it over them, and their great ones are tyrants over them. But it is not so among you; but whoever wishes to become great among you must be your servant, and whoever wishes to be first among you must be slave of all."

The disciples of Jesus were not to practice politics through the use of coercive power, but through servanthood.

Powers of Preservation and Love

Early Christians lived out Jesus' admonitions to practice a politics of servanthood. It can be seen, for example, in the way they stood against infanticide. They did this by not leading marches on Rome, nor by making contributions to sympathetic senators. They picked up "exposed" babies (babies who were left outside to die) and adopted them into their own families. Girls, in particular, were often the victims of "exposure." The vast majority of people at the time were poor, and having too many girls was perceived as an economic liability. By faith, Christians took on these "liabilities" and supported each other as they raised these rescued and adopted family members.

Sociologist Rodney Stark, in his intriguing book *The Rise of Christianity*, explains how this practice increased the number of Christians. Christian families grew larger, and those who were adopted tended to become strong Christians themselves. As men married these Christian women—women embedded in these strong social networks—the men tended to convert.

As part of Stark's quest to explain Christianity's rapid growth, he also documents how Christians in the second and third centuries cared for those sick with the plague. Rather than fleeing the plagued cities, Christians saw it as their duty to stay and take care of the sick. Modern medical experts estimate that simple nursing for plague victims (providing food, water, warmth) could have cut the mortality of epidemics by two-thirds or more. Christians helped each other and their neighbors survive in numbers that must have seemed miraculous. (And their occasional deaths witnessed to the strength of their faith that death was not final). Many converted, attracted by the strong ethic of care and mutual support that Christians lived out.

While I was in college, as thousands of gay men were dying of the AIDS epidemic, I wondered: What if Christians were the first to serve? What if, in those early days before it was known how AIDS was transmitted, Christians became known for providing nursing care? Though there were some Christians who did exactly this, what the world saw were prominent Christian evangelists pronouncing AIDS to be God's judgment on the "homosexual lifestyle."

But what if the church lived out a politics of invitational self-sacrifice, rather than power-plays and condemnation? Can we imagine a different way of doing politics?

Questions for Discussion

1. Why might using the power of politics to dictate how others live be a problematic practice for Christians?

2. What would "a politics of servanthood" look like? How might Christians practice such a politics in relation to the political controversy over homosexuality?

8

Ekklesia: A Community of Blessing

"Christianity entered history as a new social order, or rather a new social dimension. From the very beginning Christianity was not primarily a 'doctrine,' but exactly a 'community.' There was not only a 'Message' to be proclaimed and delivered, and 'Good News' to be declared. There was precisely a New Community, distinct and peculiar, in the process of growth and formation, to which members were called and recruited. Indeed, 'fellowship' (koinonia) was the basic category of Christian existence."

—Georges Florovsky

Discerning God's Way in Love

Jacque Ellul, in his book *Living Faith*, suggests that the Bible is not a big book of answers, but one that poses a huge question to us all: Will you live by faith in God?[1] Christians do not live perfect lives because we have all the right answers. Rather, what God was doing in Israel, and what Jesus proclaimed in his gospel concerning the kingdom of God, is that *God's people are to model a different social, economic, spiritual, and political life based on faith in God in order to redeem and bless the world.* Yet most Christians act as if Christianity gives us direct access to the knowledge of good and evil—and if we are good Christians, we will use economic, social, and political power to make others

---

1. Ellul, *Living Faith*, 101.

43

behave. How much better if we, as Christians, model a politics that demands we pay the cost of living a life of faith, and in so doing show the world the goodness and beauty of such a life.

The very word for church, *ekklesia,* has its roots in the political realm. The word was coined in Athens, Greece as that city-state experimented with democracy. The *ekklesia* referred to the gathering of citizens who voted on and decided how to live together as a city *(polis)*. This term also explains the most basic meaning of the word politics: *the way a group lives together.*

By understanding "politics" in this way, almost all of the Torah (Genesis to Deuteronomy) and the epistles to the churches in the New Testament are about politics. The Torah instructs Israel, and the epistles instruct the church, on how to live together. The epistles go on and on about how Christians are to live with each other in love, unity, reconciliation, humility, forgiveness, peace . . . The Bible teaches us that politics is transformed from the practice of using power to get our way to a process of lovingly trying to discern together God's way.

A New of Way of Life

We live in the shadow of Constantine, the Roman Emperor who dreamt that he would conquer his enemy by the sign of the cross. After winning a great battle, he issued the Edict of Milan and established tolerance for Christianity. Thus began a complicated history in which Christians helped form laws for the state. As a result, Christians often saw themselves as being in charge of public morality.

But such days are over. In Europe and North America, Christians are but one group among many. While some Christians may mourn this, it is also a great opportunity to return to the vital practices of the earliest Christians. Rodney Clapp summarizes the practice of the early church in this way: "The original Christians, in short, were about creating and sustaining a unique culture—a way of life that would shape character in the image of their God. And they were determined to be a culture, a quite public and political culture, even if it killed them and their children."[2] The earliest Christians didn't try to impose their morality on an unbelieving empire, but rather chose to live in life-giving ways with each other so that the world would take notice. Thus non-Christians didn't see Christians as being "against" them, but rather as inviting them into a new and different way of life.

---

2. Clapp, *Peculiar People*, 82.

How might we do politics with each other in a way that reflects the servant-politics of Jesus? How might the church demonstrate a "new way" in its conflict around homosexuality that witnesses to and blesses the world?

To ask such questions—believing there might be good answers—might seem hopelessly naïve. But I think I've seen it lived out in a small but real way in the context of church community.

A Body Politic

In the early 1990s, during my first years at the Church of the Sojourners, the community and I thought hard and argued long about homosexuality. I began reading books from the affirming side and shoving them into the hands of others. We had long meetings talking about the topic.

At one of the last meetings, I began to give yet another speech about what I was learning and what I thought we should decide. One of the older women commented, "We've already heard from you time and time again. Are we sure we want to spend more time on this?" But others intervened, and once again the whole community chose to go through the difficulty of figuring out how to live together.

In addition to dialoguing with the community and reading more on the topic than ever before, I was volunteering on the local hospital AIDS ward, had joined ACT-UP (an activist group advocating for people with AIDS), was attending worship services at an affirming church, and had begun dating a man. Given my background, I had thought gays and lesbians must be marginalized misfits. But Ignatius, the man I started dating, defied my stereotypes. He had graduated from a prestigious law school and was helping craft legislation at city hall. He had a sincere faith, a keen intelligence, a happy soul, and a zealous commitment to social justice. I could imagine a good life with Ignatius.

Eventually, it became clear that the church community needed to make a decision about homosexuality: would we affirm same-sex couples in our midst? In retrospect, I realize that because we were deciding on how we were going to live together, we were engaging in politics.[3]

Some people might find it offensive that we would decide as a group what I would do. But Scripture sees our sexual lives as implicating one another. The Apostle Paul addresses questions of sexual morality by asking, "Do you not know that your bodies are members of Christ?" (1 Cor 6:5). He continues in chapter 12, "For just as the body is one and has many members, and all the

---

3. As noted earlier, the word *politics* comes from the Greek *polis*, which most literally means "city." It has to do with how any group orders its life together.

members of the body, though many, are one body, so it is with Christ" (1 Cor 12:12). Or as Paul writes in Romans, "we are members one of another" (Rom 12:5). We are a body politic.

Though we've been trained to think about our bodies as private property, Scripture teaches us that we are connected and we affect each other. We are not each little Jesus Christs in the world, but connected to one another, we form Christ's body, with Christ as the head. As a friend of mine had tattooed on his back, we are "Property of Jesus Christ,"—and, I might add, "and to one another."

As Lauren Winner provocatively writes in her book *Real Sex,* "sex is communal." She explains this to mean that we need to encourage

> Christians to speak to one another—not just about sexual *sin,* but about all the complicated emotional and physical thickets one can find oneself in when one is having sex. It is to urge Christians to speak frankly to one another about the realities of chastity, about the thrills and tediums of married sex, about the rich meanings inherent in being sexual persons who live in bodies. It is to ask the church to serve as narrator, reminding ourselves who we are and why we do what we do.[4]

If I believe my body belongs to the larger body of Christ, then it seems right to me that we, as a community of believers, made a decision about homosexuality together. But coming to unity on that decision was difficult. Some among us believed that the Bible clearly prohibits same-sex relationships. Others believed the Apostle Paul hadn't envisioned faithful, same-sex relationships of equals—and therefore God might affirm such relationships. We couldn't agree and so we were stuck.

We did know, however, that our original vision for living in the Mission District of San Francisco was to minister to Salvadoran refugees. As we talked about it, it seemed to us that affirming same-sex relationships would be a stumbling block to many of those we wanted to care for, and so we made the practical decision not to affirm same-sex relationships in our midst. We also made the decision that even though we wouldn't practice the affirmation of same-sex relationships in our midst, we weren't making a pronouncement on the morality of homosexual practice. That is a subtle distinction, but an important one.

As I've shared that decision with other Christians, few have been satisfied with it, including some newcomers to the Church of the Sojourners. From both the left and the right, people have told me we should have figured out

---

4. Winner, *Real Sex,* 59–60.

the "right" thing to have done. Never mind that insisting on the "right" thing would have most likely split the congregation.

Yet figuring out the "right" Christian stance regarding same-sex relationships is harder than either the right or left generally admit. As it was, by faith, we tried to discern what God was up to in our midst. As far as we could tell, God was primarily using us to welcome persecuted Salvadoran refugees. It seemed to us that becoming an affirming congregation would have been a distraction from that. Of course we could have been wrong on several counts. But such is the life of faith. There are no guarantees we are "right." Rather, we trust if we make wrong decisions "in good faith," God will work for the good in spite of us.

What interests me is how this form of politics—people sorting out how to live together at a congregational level—can in practice be so rewarding and empowering. This form of politics eschews a hierarchy that uses its power to impose its will on those below. Yes, in the church we had affirmed leaders, but we hadn't chosen them on the basis of charisma, nor on the strength of how much money they had raised for an electoral campaign. We chose them on the basis of gifts. Those who were "servants of the word" were asked to speak to us from Scripture. Those who had compassionate, pastoral hearts helped shepherd us through the process of working as a group. Those among us with administrative gifts provided a structure for the decision-making process.

Because our decision-making process involved a small group of people, we knew we weren't discussing abstract principles, but actual people. The cost of what people eventually decided had obvious consequences for me. (If I decided to stay in the community, I would need to be celibate.) And because that cost was obvious, it inspired people to make the costly commitment to live as family to me and to accompany me along the way.

The decision we made may hardly seem worthy of a big word like *politics*. But as Stanley Hauerwas points out:

> Too often politics is treated solely as a matter of power, interests, or technique. We thus forget that the most basic task of any polity is to offer its people a sense of participation in an adventure. For finally what we seek is not power, or security, or equality, or even dignity, but a sense of worth gained from participation and contribution to a common adventure. Indeed, our "dignity" derives exactly from our sense of having played a part in such a story.[5]

Once we made the decision not to affirm same-sex relationships in our midst, we realized that the decision hadn't divided us, but had helped us reaffirm our

5. Hauerwas, *Community of Character*, 13.

commitment to a larger, costly adventure. We wanted to live out a new culture so we could welcome refugees. We wanted to invite people not just to become good American consumers (of things and people), but rather disciples—kingdom of God citizens.

As we continue to figure out how to live with one another, we've gone from calling our meetings "business meetings" to calling them "discernment meetings." We realize more and more that the objective is to show up wanting God's will rather than scheming about how our own will might be done. As part of that, we spend more time in prayer than we used to. It's a politics that takes on a whole new spirit, a politics that is hopefully animated by the Spirit.

Citizens of God's Kingdom

This adventure of participation in making visible God's kingdom—God's new family, economy, and politics—offers all of us a new identity. Our dignity doesn't primarily have to do with being slave or free, Greek or Gentile, male or female, gay or straight, conservative or liberal. Instead, we are offered an identity that makes us all citizens of God's kingdom working for a common goal.

I suspect this is a liberating word for us LGBT folks. As an embattled minority, it is tempting to make our sexuality our primary identity. In a culture that values radical individuality, our sexuality makes us different—and this particular difference is often what we've had to struggle with the most.

But as Michel Foucault, the godfather of queer theory, argues in his book *History of Sexuality*, sexual identities are based on doubtful Western constructs of reality.[6] For instance, Freud's idea that the libido is the source of our deepest human drive, and by understanding it we gain the deepest knowledge of ourselves, is questionable at best. Foucault believes that as we adopt sexual identities, we become prey to all kinds of power manipulations by the state, business, and others. Labeling ourselves as "gay," "bi," "queer" and so on simply allows the powers that be to fit us neatly into database fields in order to tell us how to vote and what to buy.

When we are baptized, we become adopted citizens of God's kingdom, and all other identities become secondary. Thus through my journey with the Church of the Sojourners, I discovered that my sexuality did not define me.

In the conservative church, being gay made me suspect. Was I qualified for leadership given the criteria in the pastoral epistles? Should I be trusted with children? In liberal circles, I was encouraged to see myself as part of a victimized minority. I felt boxed in and patronized. I sometimes felt the usual

6. Foucault, *History of Sexuality*, 156.

ethics demanded of straights concerning sexual ethics and fidelity were not applied to me.

I think we get beyond such boxed-in identities at the Church of the Sojourners because our lives intersect enough for us to discover our true identities as beloved sons and daughters of God. The power of the adventure brings us together in ways that transcend the identities that otherwise might separate us. In the rough and tumble of community life, our preconceived ideas about one another usually take a back seat to more basic questions: Are you someone who does your chores? Do you serve others, or are you mostly about entertaining yourself? When times get tough, do you pitch in or make things worse by complaining and griping? Do you know yourself to be lavishly loved by God and do you communicate the love of God to others?

As far as I can tell, a truly *Christian* conservative ethic requires gays and lesbians to remain celibate or marry a person of the opposite sex.[7] On the other hand, a truly *Christian* liberal sexual ethic means lifelong faithfulness for gay couples. Both of these ethics are difficult. They are difficult for heterosexuals, and perhaps even more so for homosexuals.[8] If so, how do we create a context that makes these difficult ethics more possible? Can we become church communities that support and enable the difficult ethics of Jesus?

After my church community decided not to affirm same-sex relationships, I could have opted out. I was still in a good relationship with my boyfriend. While many factors went into my decision, I eventually decided to participate in the adventure that the Church of the Sojourners offered me. The community was and is a demanding project that requires all of our imagination, effort, and gifts in order to construct a familial, economic, and political reality that witnesses to the world that the kingdom of God is at hand. I chose to remain with this church community and eventually took a vow of celibacy.

I was able to imagine celibacy not only being possible, but good, in the context of community. It meant a life without sex, but not without love. It meant a life without a nuclear family, but not without sisters and brothers, elders and children, neighbors and friends in abundance. I was loved and challenged to love.

---

7. Given the history I've related, a minority of Christian gays and lesbians will be "healed" of their orientation. Some gays and lesbians might choose to marry the opposite sex even if their orientation hasn't changed. I have married friends who are in such relationships, where both know of the same-sex attractions of one partner. Such relationships are more possible in the context of a robust church community.

8. Social support is an important factor for stable marriages. Since gays and lesbians do not generally enjoy the same marital, economic, social, and political supports as heterosexuals, I suspect gay marriage might be more difficult.

At the same time, I couldn't help but wonder about the road we didn't take. What if the community had made the decision to affirm same-sex relationships? What if my boyfriend had been open to living communally?

Water to Swim In

Can robust church communities help gays and lesbians better live out the difficult vows of marriage? Since it is true that gays and lesbians generally don't enjoy the same social, political, economic, and spiritual support for their relationships that heterosexual married couples enjoy, could healthy church communities make such an ethic more possible?

Living in community, I have seen the reality of married life up close. As wonderful as some marriages are, almost all of them go through difficult patches. It has been an honor to come alongside brothers and sisters during hard times. Usually, with others cheering them on, encouragement to get necessary help, and a strong commitment to fidelity, we've seen marriages make it through the rough spots. The Church of the Sojourners has generally (with some exceptions) been a good place for marriages. And so I suspect that if the Church of the Sojourners had made the decision to become an affirming congregation, its robust body life would have made it a particularly good place for gay and lesbian couples, too.

But few such places exist. As it stands now, both sides of the church continue to spout a lot of rhetoric about how homosexuals should live their lives while the actual practices of our churches do little to make the rhetoric possible. Do most conservative churches honor singleness and provide a healthy and vibrant body-life that makes celibacy thinkable for gays and lesbians? If not, we are being hypocrites. Do most liberal churches provide the mutual support and accountability that makes a lifelong fidelity for gays and lesbians more achievable? If not, we are being hypocrites. Because most churches *don't live in a way that makes the ethic they are espousing possible,* our churches are asking people to swim in air rather than providing the water to make swimming possible.

Though most Christians will not move into an intentional church community, our church communities, on both the right and left, can live out a body life that makes a Christian ethic for gays and lesbians more attainable. I'll explore what this might look like in chapters 11 and 12. As we move toward a thicker body-life with each other, living Christianly will become more possible for all of us: gays and straights, singles and married, conservatives and liberals.

Before we get there, though, I hope this debate helps us think more deeply about the purpose of sex, which I'll explore in the next chapter. Because we live in the sexualized, modern world, this conversation may give us better answers for what a Christian sexual ethic entails.

Questions for Discussion

1. What does it mean for the church to have "its own politics"?

2. How might the members of your church do better at practicing a truly Christian politics in their life together?

3. Why might a healthy practice of local church politics matter in the conflict around homosexuality?

9

Biblical Sexuality: An Occasion for Joy

"The mind's road to God always begins in the sexual appetite."

—Saint Bonaventure

Towards a Theology of Sex

After my anonymous encounter in the adult bookstore, I felt guilty and ashamed and began to wonder if I should take literally Jesus' admonition to "cut off" the member of my body that was causing me to stumble. At other times I wondered if I should give up on Jesus, since the Christian sexual ethic caused so much guilt and shame. But I continued on in faith and, looking back, I can see God was at work even in that difficult summer.

I made friends with Dan, a good-looking, emotionally open guy who was living with another missionary family while studying social work at San Francisco State and working two jobs to save money. We stayed up late talking about our conservative Baptist upbringings, and we found ourselves laughing a lot when we were together.

Dan came home late one night after getting up at four to work a morning shift for UPS and then a full day as a bike messenger. As he dragged his bike up the stairs, he said, "My brake wire snapped and so have I." A simple, obvious, appealing thought came into my head—I could fix it for him.

As I leaned into loving Dan, I found myself suddenly scheming to serve. All the Christian admonitions I had grown up with—be generous, caring,

52

considerate, other-focused, patient, kind—were becoming my joyful passion. I realized: *This is what I was made for. I love loving.*

Sometimes I stayed the night at Dan's house. As he got up to face his demanding twelve-hour day, I wanted to get up and embrace him, kiss him, and bless him. But I didn't. Dan was straight, and I knew he would not experience four a.m. morning-breath kisses from another guy as a blessing. But as he left I lay there fantasizing—avoiding sexual fantasies out of respect for Dan—that if I could live with Dan, adopt children with Dan, grow old with Dan (or, rather, a gay version of Dan), then my life would be wonderfully *good.*

This was the emotional beginning of the questions that haunted me. Why was it wrong to love another man? What evil would ensue if I were to marry a gay man like Dan? Loving Dan, I felt like I was living as a better version of myself. What was wrong with that? If same-sex relationships were wrong, I wanted to know why they were wrong.

I knew about the seven verses in Scripture that appear to condemn homosexuality. There are verses in both the Old and New Testaments that prohibit various things, and yet we ignore them because they are so obviously culturally specific. Some of us get tattoos (prohibited in Lev 19:28). The women in my church don't wear head coverings (1 Cor 11:5). Moreover, I was vaguely aware of the scholarship suggesting that the verses about homosexuality, given the cultural context of the time, were meant to prohibit same-sex pederasty and prostitution.

Rather than live an unexplained legalism based on a handful of possibly culture-specific verses, I began to investigate the Christian tradition concerning sexual ethics. As I did so, I stumbled into the church's historic teaching concerning sex. While some of it seemed anti-body and repressive, much of it was surprisingly . . . sexy. This teaching helped me make sense of attraction and the yearnings I feel, and it gave me a vision for experiencing my sexuality as an "occasion of joy."[1]

By faith I believe that the debate about same-sex relationships is a gift that invites the church to think well about a theology of sex. Unwrapping this gift may require some hard thinking and lead us through conflict, but what we receive as a body will be worth it.

Reflecting God's Image through Unitive Sex

Christianity witnesses that sex creates a deep union between human beings. Genesis 1:26a–29a says:

1. Rowan Williams, "The Body's Grace," 59.

> Then God said, "Let us make humankind in our image, according to our likeness . . ." So God created humankind in his image, in the image of God he created them; male and female he created them. God blessed them, and God said to them, "Be fruitful and multiply, and fill the earth and subdue it."

This is a key passage for understanding biblical sexual ethics. Christian readers of these verses have delighted in this foreshadowing of the Trinity. God (singular) says, "let us" (plural) create humankind according to our image. The grammar reflects the later Christian understanding that God is both one and three. The Father was creating through Jesus as the Spirit of God was hovering over the waters.

But how are humans to reflect God's image? Humans are created as different, and yet are meant to come together in the sexual act to be fruitful and multiply. Like the Father, Son, and Holy Spirit, who live as a community, humans are meant to come together in a profound unity. Thus Christianity declares that sex is not just a recreational activity, but is meant to *bring two different people together into a committed, loving unity.*

Theologians speak of God's *perichoresis*—a type of fellowship in which the Father, Son, and Holy Spirit embrace and permeate one another. As theologian Marguerite Shuster points out, it is a theological mistake to think of the three persons of the Trinity as existing separately or alongside each other.[2] Rather, the persons of the Trinity mutually indwell each other, or inter-penetrate each other. Described this way, we might even venture the metaphor that God lives as a sexual unity.

Scripture intimates that at the heart of reality, there is a three-personed God who lives in perfect unity, and our sexuality helps us show the world what God is like. For this reason, the Christian expression of sex ought to bring individuals together into intimate union. To use the language of the tradition, sex ought to be *unitive.*

Although this witness of the Christian tradition didn't instantly answer my question, "Is it okay with God if two guys have sex?" it was a gift, for it helped me understand how my sexuality functions to remind me that *I am made to love.* In *The Holy Longing,* Ronald Rolheiser suggests a possible Latin root of the word "sex"—*secare,* which helps us understand the purpose of sex. *Secare* means to be divided, cut off, separated. Just as we can imagine a cut-off branch that yearns to be reconnected to a tree, so we have been "sexed" and have "a holy longing" to reconnect with God and others.[3]

---

2. Quoted in van Harn, ed., *Exploring and Proclaiming,* 7.

3. Rolheiser, *Holy Longing,* 193. See especially his chapter, "A Spirituality of Sexuality."

This is where the "drive" in our sex ought to take us: to fellowship and communion. Or, as Sarah Coakley says so well, "It is not that physical 'sex' is basic and 'God' ephemeral; rather, it is God who is basic, and 'desire' the precious clue that ever tugs at the heart, reminding the human soul—however dimly—of its created source."[4]

In the creation story God exuberantly calls the creation good, good, good! But then God considers Adam and recognizes that he is alone—not good! Each of the animals is brought to Adam, but none of them is found to be a suitable mate. So God creates Eve from the rib of Adam's side and the man exults, "This at last is bone of my bones and flesh of my flesh" (Gen 2:23).

After this, the writer of Genesis comments, "Therefore a man leaves his father and his mother and clings to his wife, and they become one flesh" (2:24). In a kind of poetic logic, man and woman are to reunite as one flesh because one flesh is what they came from. The final verse of the chapter notes, "And the man and his wife were both naked, and were not ashamed" (2:25). Adam and Eve see the other's different gender, but in their vulnerable, open, naked communion, they are unified. This is how humans are meant to reflect God's image. This is what sex ought to accomplish and celebrate.

The historic Christian claim that sex is and ought to be unifying is even more clear in the New Testament. Referring to the Genesis verse (2:24) about male and female becoming one flesh, Jesus comments, "So they are no longer two, but one flesh. Therefore what God has joined together, let no one separate" (Matt 19:6; see also Mark 10:9). In 1 Corinthians 6:15–16, Paul makes the case that it is inconceivable for a Christian—who is part of Christ's body—to have sex with a prostitute because "the two shall become one flesh." In Ephesians 5:28–33, while exhorting husbands to love their wives, the writer references the Genesis verse (2:24) and offers it as a reason for the husband to love his wife, for in doing so he is effectively loving his own flesh.

In a culture that focuses on the material, we struggle to understand the implications of "become one flesh." In the biblical witness, sex is not just "wiggly meats,"[5] or the "slapping together of naked bodies,"[6] but the fusing of our essences.

I remember that after having sex, as I watched the stranger leave, I felt both a surprising bond with him and a grief. The Christian tradition is onto something when it claims that a spiritual bond is created in sex. We're not just slabs of living meat. In sex our bodies intermingle, as do our very beings. Sex is sacred and mysterious. It mixes people together into a holy unity and, at its

---

4. Coakley, *God, Sexuality*, 9.

5. Klam, *Sam the Cat*, 127.

6. Armstrong, *Why Love*, 36.

best, testifies to what God is like. A Christian sexual ethic demands that we respect the unifying function of sex.

The Blessing of Knowing and Being Known

Even though I'm single and celibate, I've found this way of thinking about sex helpful. By design I am sexed, and I long for connection. Day to day, my sexuality prompts such thoughts as, "that person is beautiful" or "hot" or "gorgeous." What am I to do with such thoughts?

Noticing the beauty of others can, at its best, help motivate me toward relationship with others. The Christian witness is that our sexuality can serve as a built-in reminder system that "life is about loving and connecting with others" and not about the distractions, such as money and pleasure, we're prone to pursue.

Real relationship means seeing the other not as an object of our desire, but as a person. Noticing beauty is different than lust. Lust moves into coveting, grasping, and idolatry. If I indulge lust, then I miss the very goal of being sexual: relationship with another person.

While lust and sexual immorality are dangers, I don't want to give up being sexual. People are often hard to love. The fact that I'm attracted to others, yearning to touch and be touched, yearning to—in biblical language—know and be known, is God's good gift. The Bible tells us that about sexuality in its very first chapters.

Although I'm single, I can express my sexuality by committing and connecting myself to others through membership in the church. As part of a church, I join my body with others to form a larger body that is the bride of Christ. The sexual overtones in that language are not just incidental or accidental. Those relationships help fulfill what God created me for by sexing me.

Unitive Sex and Homosexuality

A unitive understanding of sex poses a challenge to those who advocate for same-sex relationships. In Scripture, male and female seem to be the difference unified in sex, and by uniting the two different genders, humanity truthfully expresses what God is like. Likewise, if marriage, as Ephesians 5 teaches, symbolizes the union of Christ and the church, then the two different sexes coming together seems to most adequately express that mystery.

This has been the traditional, historic teaching of the church, but recently various theologians have questioned the idea that different genders are essential to the unifying meaning of sex. Christopher Roberts, in *Creation and Covenant: The Significance of Sexual Difference in the Moral Theology of Marriage,* reviews the historical teaching and the current challenge.

The traditional view might be stated as follows. As revealed by creation and confirmed by Genesis, male and female are the two parts of a divided whole. When we bring the two sexes together into a whole through marriage, we image God. While it is difficult to define the mystery of what makes "maleness" or "femaleness," they are not the same. To try to make up that whole with two males, or two females, is a mistake—an act of human pride attempting to remake creation according to our own desires, rather than a humble submission to how things actually *are.*

Roberts surveys Augustine, Aquinas, Luther, Calvin, Barth, and Pope Paul II, among others, to show that historic Christian thought has viewed sexual difference as an essential part of our being that has its place in God's redemptive plan.

Roberts also surveys recent attempts by modern thinkers Graham Ward, Eugene Rogers, and David Matzko McCarthy to minimize the role of gender difference in imaging God. If male and female are not essential for expressing what God is like, then there is an opening in Christian ethics for same-sex unions. Rogers, for instance, argues that because Jesus was the fullest manifestation of God, imaging God cannot demand the union of male and female.

In the end, Roberts finds the arguments by modern theologians inadequate to overturn the historic agreement that same-sex unions are wrong. He warns that by minimizing the differences in our bodies, we tend toward an anti-body stance that doesn't tell the truth about the way God intends to redeem our bodies and the world.

As part of his conclusion, Roberts writes that as differences among humans go, biologists see sexual differences as the most significant. He doesn't, however, deal with the finding by biologists that more than 450 animal species exhibit homosexual behavior[7] and as much as 2 percent of the population may be intersex.[8] Facts such as these raise an interesting question.

It is fine to report that theologians throughout the ages have built a beautiful theology of sex based on the created order of two sexes—and the mating of those two sexes images God. But what if intersex and homosexual humans are part of the created order of things? In this case, it is not modern theologians who are ignoring the reality of our bodies, but rather past theologians who failed to notice the true contours of creation.

7. Bagemihl, *Biological Exuberance.*
8. Haskell, "Nature's Case."

57

Roberts acknowledges that arguing from the order of creation has potential dangers. One danger is, as John Calvin once wrote, "the human heart is a perpetual forge of idols."[9] As we look at creation, we might unconsciously interpret it in ways that confirm our favorite idols. Thus we ought to be careful of theologies that reinforce our perceived "natural order" of things (such as the often idolized "traditional family") while not accounting for how all things are new in the revolutionary named Jesus.

Part of the "newness" Christ brings is that, in Jesus, slave and free, male and female, Jew and Gentile, are reconciled. They are not reconciled by stripping each of their uniqueness and making them exactly alike, but rather they are reconciled with their differences intact—as male and female, as Jew and Gentile.

Might the same be true in relation to straight and gay people? In the church, might LGBT people be reconciled to others not by forcing them to conform to a heterosexual sexuality, but as gays and lesbians?

On one hand, it seems like lunacy to go against the inspired intellects of Christian giants such as Aquinas and Barth—to say nothing of the most apparent sense of Scripture. On the other hand, the historic teaching of the church has done great damage to me and other LGBT brothers and sisters. With so many children of the church in anguish, *something is wrong*. Perhaps it is our theology, and certainly something has been wrong with our practice.

In the next chapter, I'll talk about an appropriate humility in relation to this question and why a final answer is so difficult to know with certainty. But first, consider another huge strand in the Christian tradition is that sex is for procreation.

Reflecting God's Image through Procreative Sex

At the risk of channeling Captain Obvious, sex is for making babies. The Genesis story tells us how Adam and Eve were told to "be fruitful and multiply" (1:28). As male and female, Adam and Eve revealed God by participating in God's life-giving power: through the act of sex God generously allows humans to participate in one of the most astonishing acts imaginable—the creation of a new human being.

Augustine believed the mutual love between the Father and the Son gives life to the Holy Spirit, who is the fruit of their love. Their unity begets life. So, too, the church has historically seen children as the appropriate fruit of human love. For centuries, the church has taught that sex, and the love it expresses,

9. Calvin, *Institutes of the Christian Religion*, 55.

is not just for those who engage in it, but—like God's love—ought to give life to others. The act of sex ought to bear fruit, and the most concrete expression of this love takes the form of children. Giving birth is a straightforward way of imaging God. Sex has the goal of making babies, and Genesis bears that out. While the Spirit may not give children to everyone, a couple ought to (in principle) be open to that blessing.

As modern people with many birth control technologies, we tend to scoff at the idea that sex must be solely devoted to creating human life. Growing up Protestant, like many of my peers, I paid little attention to this historic teaching of the church. But getting to know couples deeply in the context of community, I've developed an appreciation for the church's traditional teaching. I've seen that sex for its own sake, without a vision for the way a couple's love should bless and give life to others, can be selfish and destructive.

For many people, children are a kind of challenging curriculum from God. Rearing children helps adults learn the art of love. Children bless couples and communities by helping us all keep perspective, a sense of playfulness and wonder. Children give us a reason to get up in the morning when everything else seems meaningless.

Wendell Berry expresses this beautifully.

> [The] joining of two who know, love, and trust one another brings them in the same breath into the freedom of sexual consent and into the fullest earthly realization of the image of God. From their joining, other living souls come into being, and with them great responsibilities that are unending, fearful, and joyful. The marriage of two lovers joins them to one another, to forebears, to descendants, to the community, to Heaven and earth. It is the fundamental connection without which nothing holds, and trust is its necessity.[10]

We should not ignore the wisdom in the church's traditional teaching around procreative sex.

The Blessing of Bearing Life

The traditional church teachings have helped orient me towards a healthy sexuality. Sexual desire is a gift from God that stirs us to bring forth life, which can take many forms beyond biological reproduction.

Rolheiser writes that sexuality is our hunger to be "mothers and fathers, artisans and creators, big brothers and big sisters, nurses and healers, teachers

10. Berry, *Sex*, 138.

and consolers, farmers and producers, administrators and community build-ers co-responsible with God for the planet, standing with God and smiling at and blessing the world."[11]

While I may not have biological children, as a registered nurse I can help and heal. As a Christian and pastor, I can mentor, disciple, and encourage, par-ticipating in God's good purposes for the world. When I "smile at and bless" the world, giving my life for the life of others, I am expressing my sexuality.

Understanding the procreative aspect of sex has helped me realize that even though I am celibate, I can nonetheless participate in a positive sexual-ity. I can be "sexually active" as I use my body to love others through acts of service. Expressing my sexuality in these ways helps alleviate my desire for genital sex without dismissing or ignoring the sexual desire God has given to me as a gift.

Understanding the Christian witness that sex is to be procreative can help all of us appreciate our sexuality and embrace healthy ways of living it out. But what light does this witness shed on the argument about homosexuality?

Procreative Sex and Homosexuality

If the sex act must contain the potential for making babies for it to be moral, then homosexual sex is clearly wrong—as well as a lot of heterosexual sex! At times in church history, an emphasis on the procreative aspect of sex has overshadowed the unitive aspect of sex. Because of a complex history that involved a negative view of the body, the pleasure of sex and the love it can celebrate and deepen were sometimes ignored.

Today, however, are we in danger of reversing the mistake? Because of modern challenges to the traditional view of sex, are we emphasizing the uni-tive aspect of sex to the utter neglect of the procreative aspect?

The Catholic Church continues to teach the importance of procreation in sex to the point of prohibiting artificial birth control.[12] In this view Chris-tians most fully participate in imaging God as we engage in sex that is open to the Spirit bringing about children. When we engage in sex that is cut off from the possibility of child-bearing, sex is impoverished.

Further, marriage is a sacrament, meaning that it actually accomplishes what it symbolizes: Part of the witness of marriage is that it *gives life to people,*

---

11. Rolheiser, *Holy Longing,* 196.

12. Although natural planning is allowed for sufficiently serious reasons.

while pointing toward the fire of love at the center of the universe that gives life to all creation.[13]

While this traditional perspective is tempting because of its sheer beauty, there are two objections that make it difficult to embrace.

In Genesis 1:28, God commands humankind to be "fruitful and multiply," but God also commands humans to subdue and have dominion over the earth. Later, Genesis 2:15 explains that God put Adam in the garden to "till it and keep it."

Biblical commentator Terence Fretheim writes:

> [t]he command to be fruitful, to multiply, and to fill the earth immediately follows the word of blessing and involves a sharing of the divine creative capacities. . . . But should the point arrive at which the earth appears to be filled (the definition of which would need discussion), the human responsibility in this area would need adjustment. New situations will teach new duties regarding the created order.[14]

As the world's population reaches seven billion people, the earth is filled. Not only is the earth filled, human population is in danger of overwhelming the earth, and of making life exceedingly difficult for future generations.[15] The command to fill the earth must be tempered by the command to care for and tend the earth. We must move beyond a strictly literal sense of imaging God through giving *birth* to the more general understanding of imaging God through giving *life*, in all its senses.

The second objection to the idea that openness to procreation is a central component to a morally good sexual life is that *it is never mentioned in the New Testament*. Sex is a common topic in the New Testament, thus its writers could have mentioned the lack of openness to child-bearing in relation to homosexual acts or ancient birth control practices. But it doesn't. Indeed, the New Testament seems to lean on the side of *de-emphasizing the importance of biological children*. Jesus and the Apostle Paul are more concerned with having children of faith than biological children. As I noted in previous chapters, Jesus taught the offensive idea that family consists of those who do God's will,

---

13. See the encyclical letter *Humanae Vitae* and Pope John Paul II's *The Theology of the Body*.

14. Fretheim, "Genesis," 345.

15. An important qualification here has to do with the fact that Westerners consume so much that it makes life miserable for many and damages the environment. If we lived more sustainably, we could welcome more people. Additionally, some scientific models see the world population as stabilizing. See, for instance, "Model Predicts."

rather than biological relations. In the revolutionary ethic of Jesus, recruits become more important than offspring.[16]

For Jesus, and eventually Paul, reliance on family ties for salvation was a potential stumbling block to the way of faith and obedience. Jesus's command is not "be fruitful and multiply," but "go therefore and make disciples" (Matt 28:19a). For Jesus, it is not enough to be born an Israelite, but one must be "born from above" (John 3:7). Thus the New Testament never recommends sex for the purpose of making babies, but always emphasizes making disciples.

This doesn't, of course, mean Jesus didn't love children (he did!). Nor does it mean that openness to having children isn't a great good, or that children aren't terrific blessings. But to argue that openness to children is an essential part of a holy sex life is not supported by the New Testament witness.

Imitating God's Fidelity

As I've tried to pay attention to what my sexuality is teaching me, one of the few things I've become sure of is this important truth: *God lives as a community of faithful love. God gave us our sex drive to impel (seduce?) us toward faithful, loving community with God and others.*

Any sexual ethic that minimizes the need for an individual to be faithful to a spouse, or views sex as permissible outside of a covenant relationship, fundamentally misses the Christian vision for sex. Indeed, a central teaching of both the Old and New Testaments is that God is faithful love, and we need to imitate God's fidelity.

In the Old Testament God's character is described as *hesed*. Used over 240 times, *hesed* has a range of meanings including covenant loyalty and faithful mercy. When the Psalms mention God's goodness, the content of that goodness is often God's *hesed*. For instance, Psalm 100:5 declares, "For the Lord is good; his steadfast love [*hesed*] endures forever, and his faithfulness [a related concept] to all generations."

Even though humans betray God again and again, Jesus embodied God's provision that the covenant made in the Old Testament be kept from the human side. Jesus lived in complete faithfulness to the covenant God had made with Israel, and therefore fulfilled the human promises (*hesed*) to God. In the New Testament the key word about God becomes *agape* (God's faithful love).

16. For Israel faith was a family matter. The stories of God's work and mighty acts were family stories. Converts to faith were adopted into the family of Israel. For a small, struggling group of people who believed themselves to be the bearer of God's promise for the world, the phrase "be fruitful and multiply" was a central mandate. For Israelites, the very idea of salvation was tied up with the idea of having sex to make children.

We are told that "For God so loved [*agapao*] the world that he gave his only Son" (John 3:16a). And we have a "new command"—that we are to love (*agapao*) one another (John 13:34).

These ways of relating—*hesed* and *agape*—must be made real in what we do with our sexed selves. Jesus himself speaks multiple times against divorce and adultery (Matt 5:31–32, 19:1–9; Mark 7:22, 10:2–12; Luke 16:18, 18:20) and the rest of the New Testament warns twenty-six times against "sexual immorality" (*porneia*), which most likely includes promiscuity.

When I was considering committing myself to the community at the Church of the Sojourners, the words of Pastor Rich Reed struck me: "This is the way you grow up. You make promises and then go through the pain of keeping them."[17] That has been my experience of community, and I believe it is the experience of those who marry.

The difference between sexual consumption and sexual communion is the marriage promise. Wendell Berry explains it this way,

> What must we do to earn the freedom of being unguardedly and innocently naked to someone? Our own and other cultures suggest that we must do a lot. We must make promises and keep them. We must assume many fearful responsibilities and do much work. We must build the household of trust.[18]

One pastor suggests that just as communion remembers and celebrates God's new covenant with us, sex remembers and revels in the marriage covenant. Sex is a way of saying with one's body, "I'm remembering and keeping and celebrating my promise to you."

I realize that the ethic of restricting sex to the marriage covenant can seem excessively demanding. As I explain in earlier chapters, our consumer culture pushes us toward meeting our sexual needs in whatever way we see fit and toward seeing a partner as dispensable if he or she no longer makes us happy.

As a single person I've failed at this ethic, and at times, my sexual yearning seems so strong that such an ethic seems almost cruel. But I've also seen this ethic produce extraordinary goodness.

Jack, my mentor, divorced his first wife and floundered in his second marriage. One day he had a revelation. He realized God had given him the "perfect wife" to make him into the man God wanted him to be. Jack started calling his wife "perfect wife." Over time, as he lived into that realization, he came to love his wife better, and their marriage improved. Perseverance in his

17. Happily there is also abundant joy in the keeping of such promises.

18. Berry, *Sex*, 168.

marriage taught him more about grace, patience, forgiveness, and love than he could have learned otherwise. It was central in making him into a holy man.

I don't mean to minimize the pain of living without a sexual relationship (I know that pain deeply!) or the pain of living within a difficult marriage. Living in community, I've seen that marital dynamics can be incredibly complex—and at their worst, deeply damaging. But the Christian tradition invites us into disciplines that can help us develop a Christ-like, self-giving love. The way of celibacy and the way of faithful marriage require faith, but as we lean into them, God shows up—and we grow up.

Both celibacy and marriage are possible ways of living out a Christian sexual ethic. But is the way of marriage open to same-sex couples? The answer to this question is ultimately a matter of faith rather than certainty. This may seem like an odd claim, given how strongly I've argued for celibacy or monogamous marriage as the only Christian options. But humility is essential as we wrestle with the question of same-sex marriage.

Questions for Discussion

1. What does it mean that Christian sex ought to be "unitive"? How might that teaching be a blessing for you and others?

2. What does it mean that Christian sex ought to be "procreative"? How might that teaching be a blessing for you and others?

3. Have you seen positive examples of people (married or single) who live out "covenant fidelity"? If so, how has that encouraged you?

1 0

Walking Humbly with God

"We do not see things as they are; we see things as we are."

—Talmud

Some time ago, I looked out the front window of my San Francisco house to see two young, masculine, good-looking guys riding side-by-side on bicycles. An old pattern of thought slipped into my mind: "They are too masculine and good-looking to be gay." And then they reached out their arms, joined hands, and sailed down the street hand-in-hand. My heart leapt with joy at seeing something so spontaneously beautiful.

In response to C. Norman Kraus's argument for affirming same-sex couples, Richard Kauffman writes about the "yuck factor."[1] When some people see public displays of affection between homosexuals, their gut reaction is "yuck!" How are people to interpret that feeling? Is it a God-given instinct that tells them what is right and wrong? Or is it a socially and culturally conditioned response?

Yuck?

When I first encountered postmodernist theory—that truth is harder to know than we once thought—I reacted against it, fearing it would lead to moral relativism, where it becomes impossible to distinguish good from bad. Yet I

1. Kraus, *On Being Human*, 103.

eventually came to understand the truth of the postmodern insight that different people, in good faith, experience and interpret similar realities differently. One person reacts with a "yuck" when she sees two men kissing. Another person reacts with indifference at this sight. Yet another reacts with a leaping heart.

Postmodernism helps us humbly recognize that truth is not "right there" for the taking. Rather, we interpret things through the lens of our upbringing, education, culture, religion, class, gender, ethnicity, and sexual orientation. Thus we've got to be careful about our presuppositions and interpretive lenses before asserting something is "true." Postmodernism helps us admit that sometimes our declarations about truth are power moves designed to help us feel superior to or control others. The antidote to this power grab is humility.

As Christians, we humbly admit that our entire way of seeing is based on faith. We believe God is at work in the world, and through eyes of faith, we can see little signs of God's kingdom being made visible in the world. None of what we "see" can be proven as a mathematical formula. Rather, a Christian's way of understanding the world and morality demands faith—a leap beyond certainties and proofs. Ironically, as Christians we are often arrogant in our assertions that we have access to certain truth.

Humble Faithfulness

Ernest Becker, in his Pulitzer Prize-winning book *The Denial of Death,* helps us understand why humans—and religious people in particular—can be so arrogant. Becker explains that we are gods who poop. We have minds that can think back to the beginning of the world and contemplate concepts such as eternity, thus we experience time like gods. Yet, as we perform the basic functions of ingesting food and then piling up waste, we are reminded that we inhabit animal bodies and will die, decay, and stink. As we inhabit our decaying and dying animal bodies, we feel short-lived and insignificant.

This creates what Becker identifies as the basic human dilemma: how can we get beyond our animal bodies and be like gods?

Becker proposes that humans find symbolic ways of joining "immortality projects." If we can connect with an eternal cause, then we *feel* as if we are going to live forever. If we can link ourselves to "justice," or "God's plan for the world," or "righteousness," then we *feel* as if we've become immortal. Some people might carve their names in a redwood tree while others might join the Sierra Club. Both acts are—among other things—symbolic ways of grasping at longevity and importance.

While carving your name in a tree won't offer eternal life, by becoming a Christian we can reconcile this basic dilemma of our humanity: that we are gods who poop. When we become Christians, *we are given the gift of eternal life*, yet we often continue to *feel* our lives are unimportant and short-lived. Thus, Christianity can become a means of grasping at self-importance and godhood.

We might become a missionary, join a Christian commune, or take a strong stand on a social issue such as homosexuality (either way) in order to distinguish ourselves as superior, a cut above the rest of the herd. In this way, we make ourselves god-like by being "right," and this becomes our *alternative means of salvation, in which we don't need the real God.*

We need to repent of this plan of salvation and relinquish the hero projects we've created to shape ourselves into mini-gods. We need to recognize we are finite, dependent creatures who are lost apart from God's mercy and grace. Only then can we live gratefully into a humble obedience concerned with accomplishing God's good purposes in the world. If we are going to live beyond death's door, it will not be because we made ourselves important or "got it right." Rather, in spite of all the ways we get it wrong over and over again, God continues to extend grace to us.

Humility and the Enlightenment

To simplify a complex history, European thinkers, reacting to various events, such as thirty years of devastating religious wars and the Great Lisbon earthquake, began to seek a way of knowledge based entirely on what can be known through the senses—a "scientific method" for understanding. This was a shift from the previous idea that understanding begins with "the fear of the Lord" (Ps 111:10).

The scientific method made people healthy through advances in medicine, explained the movement of the stars in the heavens, and revealed the mysteries of the natural world. Given all the progress that took place in the sciences without reference to God and the Bible, Christians eventually confronted the difficult question: why should anyone bother with truth claims from Scripture?

Two primary answers emerged. Those thinkers who came to be known as "liberals" claimed that while Scripture consists of stories that are not necessarily true in all their details, the stories contain true revelations into the nature of humans, the world, and God. These "universal truths" would be shown to be compatible with science. On the other hand, those thinkers who came to be known as "conservatives" asserted that the biblical stories would all turn out to be true even in their particulars, and Scriptural accounts of things such as the creation could be trusted as science.

This history sets up both sides to put forth arrogant and misguided claims concerning issues such as homosexuality. On the left, the disregard of the particulars of Scripture has meant that liberal Christians are often overly open to "universal" ideas claiming the authority of science. On the right, the insistence on seeing the particulars of Scripture in scientific terms has meant that conservative Christians are susceptible to mistaken interpretations of Scripture that disregard the overall story and context.

Humility and Homosexuality

The conflict around homosexuality has been made difficult by our desire to feel superior, important, and god-like. By claiming we have certain access to the knowledge of good and evil (Gen 3:4) we assert our god-like status, turning the conflict into a shrill, difficult, and divisive debate that is splintering and fracturing the church. In such a climate, it is difficult for us to hear one another, let alone have real, generative conversations.

In the next two chapters I'll explore the specifics of how the legacy of the Enlightenment misshapes the arguments of both sides, and avoids the humility of faith.

Questions for Discussion

1. What does it mean for us to seek salvation through "being right"? How does this affect the tone of the debate around same-sex relationships?

2. How would your own life be different if you were to give up immortality projects and relax into God's gift of eternal life?

11

A Humble FIRE

"There are truths we do not see when we adopt the language of radical individualism. We find ourselves not independently of other people and institutions but rather through them."

—Robert Bellah, et al.

John Alexander, a former pastor at Sojourners, describes four "universal" ideas that are particularly appealing to liberals.[1] These ideas are: freedom, individualism, rights, and equality (FIRE).[2] If these are ultimate goods—the essence of distilled biblical truth—than the good of same-sex relationships is a no-brainer.

If freedom is an ultimate value, we must allow others to love whoever they want. If we esteem individualism, we will praise the difference of those who are queer. If respecting rights is of utmost importance, we will affirm the right of others to marry whomever they want. If equality is paramount, then gay love is as good as straight love. Some conservatives want to argue over some pesky verses so be it, but the truth is clear. The argument is over.

1. Although this is complicated as religious conservatives have bought into these ideas as well—sometimes in particularly virulent ways. The Tea Party is a sad example of this.

2. See Alexander, "Playing with FIRE: Or, Narcissism as Sacred Duty," chapter 11 in *Secular Squeeze*, 197–219.

But while these ideas have brought about great good in the world, they are not the essence of the faith. These ideas must still be understood in the light of the entire Christian story.

"F" is for Freedom

As liberation theology has shown us, freedom and deliverance are important themes in Scripture—whether the people of God are being freed from Pharaoh or sin.

Yet shortly after freeing the Israelites from Pharaoh, God tells them that they shall no longer be slaves to Pharaoh—but to God (Deut 6:13). God then gives the Israelites the Ten Commandments and five books of law, spelling out how they are to serve God. In the New Testament, Galatians 5:13 tells us, "For you were called to freedom, brothers and sisters; only do not use your freedom as an opportunity for self-indulgence, but through love become slaves to one another."

Thus Scripture does not advocate freedom for freedom's sake. As Russian author Alexander Solzhenitsyn writes, "After the Western ideal of unlimited freedom, after the Marxist concept of freedom as acceptance of the yoke of necessity—here is the true Christian definition of freedom: restriction of the self for the sake of others!"[3] While Scripture sees freedom as a great good, it sees the true goal of freedom as the ability to do God's will.

For Christians, freedom in relation to homosexuality can't simply mean freedom to "express one's sexuality." The question still remains, "what is God's will in relation to our sexuality?"

"I" for Individualism

Anthropologists tell us that the most defining feature of the West is our individualism. In *Habits of the Heart,* Bellah writes, "Anything that would violate our right to think for ourselves, judge for ourselves, make our own decisions, live our lives as we see fit, is not only morally wrong, it is sacrilegious."[4]

Because of this mindset, many kids' movies focus on a misfit who is being pressured by a peer group to fit in. The misfit must, in spite of peer pressure to conform, learn our culture's wisdom that the highest good is to "follow your

3. Solzhenitsyn, *Under the Rubble,* 136.
4. Bellah et al., *Habits of the Heart,* 142.

heart" and "be true to yourself." As Stanley Hauerwas and Willimon write, we learn that our highest duty is to make our lives a "heroic creation."[5]

In Mary Stevenson's famous poem "Footprints," she looks back at her life walk with God and notices that sometimes there are two sets of footprints along the beach, but at other times just one. She asks God why there is only one set of footprints during some of the hardest times of her life. The punch line is Jesus' response that during the hardest times he carried her. Many Christians tend to view the Christian life as an individual walk with Jesus, where Jesus occasionally gives us a lift to help us through difficult times.

But as my friend Tim Lockie points out, there is already a story in Scripture about footprints in the sand: the Exodus of the Israelites walking through the desert from Egypt. Although there were thousands of footprints, there were not as many footprints as people. Many of the young, old, and sick, were carried by others. Unlike Stevenson's individual walk with Jesus, the biblical vision of life with God is of a community being led by God from the bondage of Empire into the goodness of a new way of life with *one another*.

In the New Testament as well, the biblical vision is not of individuals living heroically spiritual lives so that the world might see that the Messiah has come. Rather, Jesus says it will be the disciples' life together—the way they love *one another* and live in unity—that will witness to the world that the Messiah has come (see John 13:35 and 17:23). The New Testament gives instructions to churches (*ekklesia*, which literally means "the gathered") about how to live together in love and unity.

As theologian Gerhard Lohfink writes,

> The true miracle in the Church happens when humans let themselves be gathered and when they let their lives be joined into the true community; and the fact that this happens time and again in the history of the Church, in spite of everyone's desire to be his own master and in spite of everyone's wish to entrench himself behind his own four walls and that in all this these persons seek for God's will in unanimity; such is the true miracle of the Church. Where all this happens, there is the place where God is acting.[6]

If individualism is our highest duty, then "expressing ourselves" and our sexuality becomes a sacred obligation. But if we understand ourselves as part of God's people, we must ask, "How does my sexuality need to function in order to serve the community?"

---

5. Hauerwas and Willimon, *Resident Aliens*, 55.

6. Lohfink, *"Does God,"* 16.

"R" is for Rights

The Enlightenment also passed down the "universal truth" about rights. Although an autopsy of a human being will never reveal a heart, liver, and a bundle of rights, in fighting fascist governments, dictators, and torturers of all kinds, there is power in the appeal to respect "basic human rights."

In a pluralistic, democratic society, it is fair to assert that everyone ought to have equal rights. This is one of the best arguments for gay marriage.[7] The belief that marriage is between a man and a woman is usually defended on religious grounds, thus to prohibit same-sex couples from marrying is an unfair bias in favor of certain people from a particular religious tradition.

In the political realm, rights is a powerful tool, yet in everyday life, the use of "rights" language is often code for, "While I can't defend what I'm doing on moral grounds, you and/or the government can't stop me." Christians ought to think carefully about rights language, because at the heart of our faith, we see Christ choosing to give up his rights.

> Let each of you look not to your own interests, but to the interests of others. Let the same mind be in you that was in Christ Jesus, who, though he was in the form of God, did not regard equality with God as something to be exploited, but emptied himself, taking the form of a slave, being born in human likeness. And being found in human form, he humbled himself and became obedient to the point of death—even death on a cross." (Phil 2:4–8).

This passage does not instruct Christians to be abused, but cautions us to remember that the kingdom will come when we look to "the interests of others," not when we demand our rights.[8] In 1 Corinthians 9:5, Paul argues that though missionaries had the right to take a believing wife along with them, they gave up this right for the sake of the gospel.

While rights are an important concept in the political realm, they aren't a trump card when it comes to thinking Christianly about the morality of same-sex unions.

---

7. With evangelical preacher Tony Campolo, I would prefer that the state issue "civil unions" to everyone and for each church to define what it thinks of as "marriage."

8. I'm aware of the feminist critique of this and won't try to make a complete response here. At the very least, this passage is aimed at those in positions of privilege. As white, male privilege continues, those of us in that category ought to pay special attention.

"E" is for Equality

At the heart of the concept of equality is the beautiful truth that we are all equal in God's eyes—regardless of the color of our skin, the sex of our bodies, or the orientation of our sexuality.

Unfortunately, this ideal is distorted when we buy into the false idea that because we are all "equal" we don't need to listen to anyone else. If I have heart trouble, I need to listen to my cardiologist, for though we are both of equal worth, she is my superior in knowledge about hearts.

So it is with moral knowledge. If someone has thought long and well about ethics, if someone is living a saintly life, if someone is conducting a love life that nourishes and builds up others, I will do well to listen to my superiors in Christian wisdom, for I have much to learn from them.

If it comes down to a choice of listening to ourselves or Christian tradition and Scripture, we ought to listen to the latter. Of course, we will have to wrestle with the question, "what is the most truthful interpretation of the tradition and Scripture?" But we will definitely end up on the wrong track if we stubbornly follow our individual thinking just because we're "equal" with everyone else.

Some may find this critique of FIRE offensive, because these ideas have brought about so much good for women, ethnic minorities, and the LGBT community. Though these FIRE ideas can bring about great good in the world, they are not the essence of our faith and so must be interpreted in light of the entire Christian story.

If we let these ideas own our souls, we're going to end up as cogs in the modern machine—"individualists" who are, ironically, the ultimate conformists. We'll each be so detached from one another and so consumed with ourselves that we will enjoy little solidarity. We'll be so busy pursuing our own freedom, expressing our radical individualism, demanding our rights, and asserting our equality that we'll end up as separate, self-absorbed, rootless beings at the beck and call of the market with its mirages of money and prestige.

I am especially concerned about the effects that a distorted FIRE ethic might have on the church. If "equality" is my ethic, why would I ever submit myself to a church body? If my faith is in freedom, why should I ever commit to staying around for others? If individualism is my instinct, why should I make myself interdependent with others? If rights are my religion, why would I ever risk getting close enough to others to get wounded?

When I first came to Christian community and thought about joining my life with others, I had the feeling in the pit of my stomach that I was betraying my duty to myself. Happily, I came across Robert Bellah's *Habits of* the Heart: Individualism and Commitment in American Life, which helped me reach into my guts, pull out uncomfortable feelings, and name them. With Bellah's help, I realized that my culture had lit a FIRE in me, one that kept me from the kind of relationships I most deeply desired. If I would have let the logic of FIRE rule, I would have remained lonely and isolated. Instead, Bellah freed me to give myself to the family called church.

If we completely accept the logic of FIRE, then complete affirmation of same-sex relationships inevitably follows. But to think Christianly about homosexuality requires a deeper grappling with Christian tradition and Scripture than the left has done.

Realizing that the presuppositions of FIRE don't necessarily trump other arguments ought to make liberal Christians more humble about speaking the truth for God.

Questions for Discussion

1. Are there particular ways you want to celebrate and remember the good that the values of freedom, individualism, rights, and equality have accomplished? Are there ways you have seen the values of FIRE do damage to yourself or the church?

2. What would it mean to hold these values humbly?

1 2

A Humble Biblicism

"Looking to God for ad hoc *psychic direction in each situation is only a short step away from looking to Him for written rules and regulations for each situation. Both derive from a legalistic outlook, both seek to evade the responsibility of making mature decisions, and both miss the point of how God related to His people."*

—John Boykin

Conservatives also need to adopt a humble stance in approaching truth, for they often get so caught up in the particulars of Scripture that they miss the overall story: Jesus and his kingdom. Conservatives responded to the search for secure knowledge by claiming that the Bible is good scientific knowledge. Thus the Bible becomes a textbook for life with an index at the back. When confronted by a life problem or issue, we simply turn to the back, look up the relevant verses, and "Voilà!" divine wisdom is secured.

In this way, the Bible becomes a kind of "owner's manual" for life, which can be consulted if we want to be a good leader, run a business, enhance our sex life, or lose weight. Rick Warren's Saddleback Church seems to play off this mindset with its "Daniel Plan: God's Prescription for Your Health"—a diet plan based on the book of Daniel.[1] A look at Daniel 1 reveals the "plan" was a diet of water and vegetables—hardly a sustainable way of staying healthy.[2]

1. Kluger and Dias, "Does God," 40.

2. The actual "plan" offered by Saddleback is much better than that. It incorporates the best insights of modern medicine and psychology to help its members lose weight.

Scripture as Witness to Jesus

The textbook view of Scripture, known as biblicism, is explained well in Christian Smith's *The Bible Made Impossible: Why Biblicism Is Not a Truly Evangelical Reading of Scripture*. He explains the various assumptions of biblicism, which include: God's words were written down perfectly in human language; the Bible communicates everything related to faith we need to know; any reasonable human being can interpret Scripture rightly by paying attention to the plain sense of the words; we don't need others or the Christian tradition to help us interpret Scripture (*sola scriptura*); the Bible is completely, internally consistent.[3]

Yet if Scripture is plain, straightforward, and perfectly understandable for any sincere layperson, Smith wonders, why do we have endless disagreements over the atonement, eternal security, Christ's second coming, election, and so on? Surely the Bible is more complex than a simple biblicism allows.

While it is impossible to delve deeply into the argument about biblicism here, or to make a full proposal about how to interpret Scripture in a better way than biblicism permits, Smith does suggest one principle that bears repeating: all Scripture must be interpreted as pointing to Jesus. As he writes, "it is not the words of the Bible that are 'the way, the truth, and the life.' It is the person of Christ, to whom the Bible witnesses."[4]

In John 5:39, Jesus says, "You diligently study the Scriptures because you think that by them you possess eternal life. These are the Scriptures that testify about me" (NIV). Jesus is the focus of Scripture and the lens through which we are to read Scripture.

This does not deny the inspiration of Scripture or the authority of Scripture—nor does it mean taking a "liberal" view of Scripture. But it does mean seeing the Bible more as a detective story than a dictionary. Not every verse of Scripture is made to stand alone like entries in a dictionary. At the heart of the mystery, Christ is revealed, and as we read passages with the hindsight of Christ's life, death, and resurrection, they take on deeper and better meanings. Not that they were inscrutable before, but read in the light of Jesus, they make deeper and better sense.

In short, we get it wrong when the Bible is understood as a bundle of factoids dropped from heaven to make life work out. But we might get it right when we read Scripture as a story pointing to Christ.

---

3. Obviously not all conservative churches believe all of these.

4. Smith, *Bible Made Impossible*, 99.

Textbook Homosexuality

Approaching the Bible as textbook, one finds seven explicit references to same-sex sex: Genesis 19:1–9, Leviticus 18:22, Leviticus 20:13, Judges 19:22–23, Romans 1:26–27, 1 Corinthians 6:9–11, and 1 Timothy 1:10.

Genesis 19:1–9

When God sends angels to Sodom to see whether the city is as bad as the "outcry that has come to me" (Gen 18:21), Lot makes them "a feast" (19:3)—hospitality that ancient Near Eastern cultures would have venerated. In contrast to that hospitality, "the men of Sodom, both young and old, all the people to the last man," surround the house and demand to have sex with the visitors.

From a biblicist perspective, "the sin of Sodom" is perceived as homosexuality. The Sunday school flannel-graph boards of my childhood conveyed the horror of people being turned into sulfur, and I grew up thinking that this was clear evidence of God's disgust with homosexuals. I pondered the story of Sodom and Gomorrah and wondered, "Does God find me disgusting?"

But a deeper reading of this story reveals that the men of Sodom were not threatening the angels with the "sin" of homosexuality, but rather with gang rape. In the ancient world, raping another man—thus putting him in the "woman's role"—was an act of cruel humiliation. Sodom was not an ancient gay spa, but a town with married men, women, and their children.

The sin of these men was not homosexuality, but rather their brutal abuse of strangers. Their actions conveyed domination and power rather than the hospitality of Lot (and previously Sarah and Abraham). This story condemns what might be a prison rape in our day, rather than mutual love between two people of the same sex.[5] Even so, the Sodom and Gomorrah passage is used by evangelicals as evidence that homosexuality is wrong.[6]

Read through the lens of Christ, we see Abraham, an advocate for Sodom, pleading with God to spare the city, until God agrees that Sodom will not be destroyed if ten righteous people are found. Yet we are all in the same "unrighteous" category as the inhabitants of Sodom and Gomorrah. For when we turn to the New Testament, "it is written: 'There is no one who is righteous, not even one'" (Rom 3:10). As Ezekiel 16:49 reveals, "This was the guilt of your sister Sodom: she and her daughters had pride, excess of food, and prosperous

5. The passage in Judges 19:22–23 describes a threatened rape, similar to the story of Sodom. Because the context is similar, it can be interpreted as a critique against rape and domination, rather than homosexuality.

6. See, for example, Gagnon, *Bible and Homosexual*, 71.

ease, but did not aid the poor and needy." For those of us in the affluent West, this indictment strikes us all.

But thankfully, though we are all unrighteous, we have our own Abraham, Jesus—an "advocate with the Father"—who compassionately intercedes for us (1 John 2:1). Interpreting Sodom and Gomorrah through the lens of Christ's mercy is more "evangelical" than using this story to prove that God hates homosexual sex.

Leviticus 18:22, 20:30

Both Leviticus verses prohibit a man lying with another man as "with a woman." Leviticus 20:30 reads, "If a man lies with a male as with a woman, both of them have committed an abomination; they shall be put to death; their blood is upon them." For a strong biblicist, the command is clear, simple, and unambiguous.

Yet this creates problems when we consider the entire book of Leviticus. For Leviticus 20 also commands, "All who curse father or mother shall be put to death; having cursed father or mother, their blood is upon them" (9). Shall we take such a verse literally? Obviously, in the free and independent culture of the United States, we decry cultures that practice such savage death sentences.

Leviticus 20:18 reads, "If a man has sexual relations with a woman during her monthly period, he has exposed the source of her flow, and she has also uncovered it. Both of them are to be cut off from their people" (NIV). Even the most committed biblicists tend to dismiss such verses as irrelevant for our modern culture because they were tied to ancient (and now archaic) beliefs that menstruation defiled women and made them unclean.

Clearly, our modern culture interprets many of the laws in Leviticus (and elsewhere in Scripture) through the underlying reasons for the law, rather than a zealous adherence to every single law. Since the ancients believed that putting a man in "the woman's role" was the ultimate insult, it is reasonable to question whether such a law should enforced today.

New Testament Passages

While some conservative Christians might agree that the four Old Testament passages are not sufficient to condemn modern day same-sex relationships, there are three New Testament passages that seem to speak clearly about homosexuality. Yet read in their wider context, the message is not so clear.

Thus in the current debate, conservatives will need to approach Scripture with humility rather than prideful certainty.

Romans 1:26–27

This passage from Romans seems to make an ironclad case against same-sex relations:

> For this reason God gave them up to degrading passions. Their women exchanged natural intercourse for unnatural, and in the same way also the men, giving up natural intercourse with women, were consumed with passion for one another. Men committed shameless acts with men and received in their own persons the due penalty for their error.

Anyone who doesn't read this as a clear-cut condemnation of homosexuality might be accused by biblicists of not taking Scripture seriously. Interestingly, however, for the first four centuries of the early church, Christians did not interpret the passage as a condemnation of lesbianism, but rather as a condemnation of women who had anal sex with a man. Anal sex was a common form of birth control, and this act contradicted the view of the early church fathers that sex was only permissible for the sake of having children. Here is at least one case of Christians taking Scripture seriously, but interpreting it differently than modern biblicists.

As modern science reveals that some people have a "natural" inclination for a partner of the same sex, we need to wrestle with the "obvious" meaning of this passage so we might either vindicate it or come to a different understanding—precisely as a way of *taking Scripture seriously.*

The best way to arrive at a truthful understanding of this passage comes through careful attention to its context. The passage comes at the beginning of Romans, a book in which Paul is wrestling with the fact that because of Jesus, God has now grafted the Gentiles into God's people.

There is widespread agreement among commentators that Paul seems to be addressing two groups in Rome: Jewish Christians and Gentile Christians, who are at odds with one another. He is working towards encouraging them to welcome one another (Rom 15:7), and he makes the claim in chapter 10 that "there is no distinction between Jew and Greek; the same Lord is Lord of all and is generous to all who call on him" (v. 12).

Paul begins by addressing Jews, and for a moment he appears to take their side. He writes of the Gentiles who, although they saw all the wondrous works of God in creation, "exchanged the glory of the immortal God for images resembling a mortal human being or birds or four-footed animals or reptiles" (23).

The Gentiles were idolaters and Paul recounts some of the sexual practices that would have been most objectionable to Jews. James Alison describes one context—temple-cults—in which these practices took place:

> [T]he rites involved orgiastic frenzies in which men allowed themselves to be penetrated, and which culminated in some of those in the frenzy castrating themselves, and becoming eunuchs, and thus priests of Cybele, for whom, as was common with Mother Goddess cults, transcending gender was particularly important. Such castrated devotees, sometimes called "galli" would wander around, as do the "hijra" in modern India, as festal eunuchs assumed to have magic powers or prophetic gifts.[7]

This historical context makes sense of Paul's assertion that such men "received in their own persons the due penalty for their error" (27b).[8]

Paul presses on with his argument as he asserts that the Gentiles are:

> filled with every kind of wickedness, evil, covetousness, malice. Full of envy, murder, strife, deceit, craftiness, they are gossips, slanderers, God-haters, insolent, haughty, boastful, inventors of evil, rebellious toward parents, foolish, faithless, heartless, ruthless. They know God's decree, that those who practice such things deserve to die—yet they not only do them but even applaud others who practice them (29b–32).

Presumably, at this point, Paul has won over his Jewish audience. He thoroughly understands their complaints about the idolatrous, sex-obsessed, sinful Gentiles. But then the passage pivots suddenly to, "Therefore *you*." Conducting what New Testament scholar Richard Hays calls a "homiletical sting operation,"[9] Paul turns the tables and reveals his main contention. "Therefore you have no excuse, whoever you are, when you judge others; for in passing judgment on another you condemn yourself, because you, the judge, are doing the very same things" (2:1).

He has, after all, been slipping in some sins (amongst those denouncing Gentile practices) of which the Jews would have been guilty: envy, covetousness, gossip, and boasting. As Paul writes in verse 9, "There will be anguish and distress for everyone who does evil, the Jew first and also the Greek." It is

---

7. Alison, "But the Bible," para 33.

8. Or perhaps, given that playing the "woman's role" was seen as a debasement, receiving the penis itself is the "due penalty" for error.

9. Hays, *Moral Vision*, 389.

not enough for Jews to hear God's law, because it is only "doers of the law who will be justified" (2:13).

The passage turns out to be one long, clever setup to rebuke religious people for feeling superior to others. Yet ironically, this is the passage most quoted by conservative Christians to judge "idolatrous, sex-obsessed, sinful" homosexuals.

The passage is part of Paul's greater message in Romans that Jews and Gentiles need to reconcile with and love one another because of the outrageous generosity of Jesus. Romans 1:26–27, read in context, calls us to see ourselves as fundamentally equal to the outsider, to see our own sin first, to treat our brothers and sisters in Christ with humility, rather than judgment. Because of Christ's work, *Christians are called to have humility in relation to one another.*

1 Corinthians 6:9–11

The passage reads:

> Do you not know that wrongdoers will not inherit the kingdom of God? Do not be deceived! Fornicators, idolaters, adulterers, male prostitutes, sodomites, thieves, the greedy, drunkards, revilers, robbers—none of these will inherit the kingdom of God. And this is what some of you used to be. But you were washed, you were sanctified, you were justified in the name of the Lord Jesus Christ and in the Spirit of our God.

If the passage is read through a biblicist lens, without regard to the historical context, then the meaning is simple and straightforward: homosexuals aren't going to heaven. But careful attention to the context and history of the words used reveals a more complicated story.

As in Romans, Paul is addressing a situation of conflict.[10] While the writers of the epistles sometimes counsel separating from "false teachers," the overall thrust of the letters is toward unity, as it is here.

This chapter concerns the practice of some Corinthian believers taking others to court. In verse 7 Paul asks, "Why not rather be wronged?" Throughout the letter, Paul appeals to the example of Christ as the way to get through conflicts. Whether responding to lawsuits, disagreements around the gift of

10. Some might argue that the Holy Spirit makes us good people who no longer get into conflicts, yet the biblical witness recognizes conflict as an integral part of what God uses to grow us up. Paul's need to repeatedly address such conflict might give us some perspective on the current controversy in the church over homosexuality.

tongues, or whether or not to eat food offered to idols, Paul answers each disagreement with the same solution: be crucified like Christ!

Similar to the pivot we saw in Romans 1, Paul accuses the very ones who are seeking judgments against others ("you yourselves") of being those who "wrong and defraud—and believers at that" (v. 8). Paul lists concrete ways the Corinthians wrong others as "fornicators, idolaters, adulterers, male prostitutes, sodomites, thieves, the greedy, drunkards, revilers, robbers" (9b–10a).

The obvious question for a modern gay or lesbian person is, "If I give my body and soul to another person in love, how am I wronging that person, or the body of Christ? Isn't such an act in the spirit of Christ?"

Here, the ambiguity of the Greek words complicates things. The first word, *malakoi*, is translated by the NRSV as "male prostitutes," but most literally means "soft" or "effeminate" and usually referred to the passive male partner in homosexual activity. The second word, *arsenokoitai*, translated as "sodomite," is used here for the first time in all known Greek literature.

Robin Scroggs argues that *arsenokoitai*, literally "man who beds a man," is a translation of the first part of Leviticus 20:13: "If a man lies with a male as with a woman, both of them have committed an abomination" (13a).[11] Paul, as a student of Torah, probably thinks of all homosexual activity as wrong.

But why two words? Here we begin to understand the difference between our modern thinking about "homosexuals" and the way homosexuality was thought about in the ancient world. In Greco-Roman culture, it was understood that there was always an active partner and a passive partner. The passive partner—the one playing "the woman's role"—was thought of as inferior and was most likely subordinate in rank and power. At its most extreme, *arsenokoitai* might have referred to the "John" (a man who hires prostitutes) and *malakoi* to male prostitutes, as the NRSV suggests.

Given this context, the meaning of 1 Corinthians is this: stop employing power to use others for sex, because this is unjust, unrighteous, pagan behavior. The people of God do not treat each other this way because Christ has taught us not to exploit each other, but to lay down our lives for each other in self-sacrificing love.

1 Timothy 1:9–10

1 Timothy 1:9–10 also pairs "sodomite" (*arsenokoitai*) with another vice. Notice the possible connection between the words I have bracketed together:

11. Scroggs, *New Testament*, 106–8.

> This means understanding that the law is laid down not for the innocent but for the [lawless and disobedient], for the [godless and sinful], for the [unholy and profane], for those who [kill their father or mother, for murderers], [fornicators, sodomites, slave traders], [liars, perjurers], and whatever else is contrary to the sound teaching that conforms to the glorious gospel of the blessed God, which he entrusted to me.

As in our present day, the sex trade and slavery were connected. Given the context, *arsenokoitai* (translated here as "sodomite") may mean the man who uses male prostitutes, and *pornos* (translated here as "fornicator") may mean male prostitutes since the female form of *pornos (porne)* is usually translated as "prostitute." If so, then the author is condemning the unjust use of others' bodies illustrated by the slave traders and "Johns" who use vulnerable men. If this is the case, this Scripture is not a direct condemnation of the homosexual relations of love and mutuality that we know today, but rather of a degrading system of exploitation and abuse.

The Aim of Such Instruction

The discussion of "sodomites" in 1 Timothy relates to a larger discussion about those who presume to teach the law. Included in this discussion is a clear admonition for those who presume to teach: "But the aim of such instruction is love that comes from a pure heart, a good conscience, and sincere faith" (1:5).

Christians who wrestle with Scripture deeply and seriously are left with difficult questions. Do these verses that deal with murderers and slave traders also refer to people who love people of the same sex? And if I choose to admonish such a person, how is the aim of that instruction "love that comes from a pure heart, a good conscience, and sincere faith"?

Given the ways these verses have been translated into English, it is understandable that conservative Christians would take these verses as clear cut prohibitions of homosexuality. What I do wish to challenge, however, is the accusation that Christians who affirm same-sex relations "don't take Scripture seriously." In fact, an actual (versus superficial) commitment to Scripture means that even those who "take Scripture seriously" have good reasons for humility.

Experiments in Truth: The Path of Humility and Love

Because we live in a time when knowing the truth is more complicated than we used to think, all Christians are called to humility. Though Christians have sometimes acted as if we have a superpower in Scripture that gives us direct and sure access to truth, neither liberal nor conservative Christians have direct, unbiased access to Scripture.

We also need to be aware of the Pharisaic impulse to "justify" ourselves by asserting that we have the "right" opinions on issues. When we walk with superiority rather than humility, we alienate others and live as if our "right" ideas justify us, rather than God through our advocate, Jesus.

In a TED talk on being wrong, Kathryn Schulz asks the audience, "How does it feel emotionally to be wrong?" Audience members offer words such as, "dreadful, embarrassing." Schulz pauses, then says, "These are great answers, but they are answers to a different question. You guys are answering the question, 'How does it feel to realize you are wrong?' . . . But just being wrong doesn't feel like anything."[12] Or, to say it differently, it feels just like *being right*.

Christians can avoid this trap by humbly acknowledging that we *live by faith*. Faith doesn't mean, "I've got it all right," or "I've figured everything out." Rather, we trust in the goodness and grace of God. While this means we will be living with humility rather than certainty about, well, *everything*, we will never come across a better bet.

When we get beyond thinking that having the right opinion about issues is paramount and start living out "experiments in truth" in a grand adventure, others will pay attention. People will be drawn to such a faith, and we will have myriad opportunities to love and bless them.

Questions for Discussion

1. Are you ever prone to see individual verses and miss the overall story of the Bible? How does a rigid biblicism distort the message of Scripture?

2. How can we both speak the truth as we see it, and yet do so with humility?

12. Schulz, "Being Wrong."

13

A Compassionate Traditionalism

"Let your religion be less of a theory and more of a love affair."

—G. K. Chesterton

The week before writing this chapter, I got together with a forty-something gay friend who used to attend a traditional evangelical church. He poignantly and succinctly summarized his long journey of self-acceptance by saying, "God loves gay Kent."

At age eleven, Kent began wrestling with his attraction to other males. As his understanding of his sexual orientation deepened during his college years, Kent pursued the advice of Christian leaders offering him the hope of orientation change through reparative therapy, healing prayer, and dating women. Yet twenty years later, his fundamental attraction to men was unchanged. After struggling with depression and thoughts of suicide, Kent decided not to spend any more time or energy trying to change his sexuality. Instead, he turned his attention to living with full integrity as a gay man who follows Jesus.

That Kent calls himself "gay" might be difficult for many conservative Christians, and it was difficult for some members of Kent's congregation. As he became more comfortable with his sexuality, his church leaders became more uncomfortable. Kent remained single and celibate and kept that commitment in complete transparency with the pastor and select elders of his congregation. Even so, the church leadership eventually asked him to step out of his role as worship leader—a role he had performed with passion and skill for ten years.

When Kent was asked to resign his worship leader role, he left the church. Although he remains fiercely committed to loving God and continues to work with a spiritual director, he feels deeply hurt.

In this chapter, I will explore what it might look like for conservative Christians to love LGBT members of their congregations. I'm not suggesting that churches who take the traditionalist stance must change their theology. In fact, I respect the way the conservative church holds out a sexual ethic of no premarital sex and champions sexual fidelity in marriage. If the conservative church is right that homosexual sex is outside of God's good boundaries, then the most loving thing they can do is to hold out this ethic for its gay and lesbian members.

But it is clear that the traditional church has not always done well with its LGBT children. How can churches hold the traditionalist view while caring for its homosexual members? First, I will recap the traditional church's theology around homosexuality. Then, I will suggest a path toward more effective care.

How the Traditional Church is Reading Scripture with Integrity

In the previous chapter I discuss the seven verses in the Bible that address homosexuality and how these passages might not be directed at the love relationships lived by gays and lesbians today. Thus the conservative church will need to bear witness to its stance with humility.

On the other hand, there are good reasons to believe that God's vision of human flourishing excludes same-sex relations. In Romans 1, Richard Hays points out that Paul seems to link homosexual practice to ways the Gentiles violate God's intent for creation. Hays writes, "Paul's choice of homosexuality as an illustration of human depravity is not merely random; it serves his rhetorical purposes by providing a vivid image of humanity's primal rejection of the sovereignty of God the Creator."[1]

Male and female bodies fit together. Just as we observe the wings of a bird and think, "that creature is meant to fly," so too it is reasonable to observe our anatomy and think, "females and males are meant for each other."

As I note in the previous chapter, great Christian thinkers throughout the centuries have believed that in the creation account, the male-female distinction is highlighted as the most basic difference between human beings and thus our sexed status is important. When the male-female difference is

---

1. Hays, *Moral Vision*, 386.

brought together in matrimony, that union points to a greater mystery, namely that Christ and the church (different beings) are made one (Eph 5:32).

This bringing together of difference reveals a concrete example of God's nature and work in the world. The Trinity consists of three different persons living in a perfect unity. God's nature is to unify, reconcile, and knit together that which is separated. Just as Christ and the church are becoming one, so also the children of God—slave and free, Jew and Gentile, male and female—are becoming one (Gal 3:28). The traditionalist church insists on remaining faithful to the witness of bringing together *different sexes.*

Although there are few verses about homosexuality in the Bible, all the verses that mention homosexuality teach against it.[2] While two of the seven passages are embedded in Old Testament law, which Christians don't fully observe today, Paul's references to homosexuality may confirm that he upheld the Old Testament prohibitions against homosexual practice.

The plain sense of Scripture speaks against same-sex unions. If the conservative church were to compromise on this issue, would it mean that on crucial issues interpretation must be left in the hands of Bible scholars?

Even taking the view that Scripture must be read in the context of its original cultural situation, it is not clear that the resulting interpretation is an affirmative stance. While same-sex prostitution and pederasty were prominent forms of homosexual activity in the first century, "genuine love" between men may have been known to the Apostle Paul.[3] Paul may have thought that *porneia* (sexual immorality) includes any form of same-sex sexual relations.

The traditionalist church could potentially witness against the consumer culture of our age, which teaches that we will be most blessed if we follow our own will, desire, and orientation. While such a belief allows marketers to sell us tons of stuff, it is not faithful to the historic Christian witness that we are most blessed when we discover God's will for our lives and do it.

---

2. A possible exception to this, though highly contentious, is the account of the love between Jonathan and David. For one treatment of this see Knust, *Unprotected Texts,* 39–42.

3. Thiselton, citing Christian Wolff, in *First Epistle to the Corinthians,* 452. Paul may have known of Pausanias of Athens and the tragic poet Agathon, who were adult male lovers. There is, however, controversy among scholars as to how common this practice was and whether it was venerated (as were certain forms of homosexual pederasty) or mostly ridiculed—as in the comedies of Aristophanes (because to be "penetrated" as an adult male was seen as shameful). See Paris, *End of Sexual,* for a convincing argument that the construct of homosexuality we have today cannot be easily imposed on first-century culture.

But the conservative church has not done a good job at showing homosexuals the way to blessedness. Retired Bishop Gene Robinson describes the feeling he got from his church when he was growing up.

> Without ever speaking the word *homosexuality,* its members made clear what God thought of people who were "that way." I didn't know exactly what sodomy was, but I knew that the penalty for it was condemnation and death. Being an "abomination" sounded totally beyond God's love.[4]

So many gay Christians report feeling depressed and even suicidal due to the messages they receive from church.[5]

How can the traditionalist church do well by homosexuals? As the saying attributed to Morton Kelsey goes, "The church is not a museum for saints but a hospital for sinners." Unfortunately, in the past, LGBT people have often experienced the church as a place that teaches secrecy and shame. The challenge is how to care for LGBT people without imparting a "hospital acquired illness"—that is, to care for them without doing more harm.

Reflecting on my own experience growing up in the conservative church, I urge traditionalist churches to embrace the following five practices as they journey with LGBT people in their midst.

One: Affirm LGBT People as Body Members

A couple of years ago, a friend put a man named Don in contact with me. Don served as a missionary for a conservative denomination, is married to a woman, and has four children. At age sixty-three, after denying that he was gay for most of his adult life because of shame and fear, he came to accept his same-sex attraction. He believes God is calling him to remain faithful to his marriage, but to be honest about his orientation.

Don isn't looking for any kind of sexual relationship with a man. His wife loves him, knows of his orientation, and continues to be enthusiastic about their marriage. To any outsider Don appears to be a happily adjusted heterosexual man.

Yet Don contacted me because he was desperate to talk about the pain of self-delusion he had practiced on himself and the ways he had deceived others in order to maintain his straight appearance. Don hadn't told most members of his congregation about his orientation for fear of being judged.

---

4. Gold and Drucker, *Crisis,* 26.

5. See ibid. for more examples of this.

I know there are many varieties of Don in traditional congregations. There is the gay teen, wondering if all the "wait 'til marriage" talk has anything to do with him, because he only has sex with guys. There is the man sitting in the pew, wiggling his toes in his brown dress shoes, which are hiding the pink polish he applied to his toenails this morning as he wrestled with his gender identity. There are the two women living as a couple with adopted children, sitting farther apart than usual during the worship service so no one will suspect the truth about their home life. While the pastor preaches against the "homosexual agenda," the youth pastor is wondering, "How am I ever going to convince his daughter to talk to him about her fear that she is lesbian?"

If you are part of a conservative church, there may be someone you know who is wondering about telling you about his or her struggle with sexual orientation. Perhaps that person is wondering how you will react, who you will tell, how will you treat him or her from now on.

Statistically speaking, in any group of thirty to fifty people, there is likely to be someone struggling with issues of sexual orientation and gender identity.[6] This must be taken into account when teaching about these issues. Church leaders who speak of "the gays" who are corrupting traditional morals are, perhaps unconsciously, communicating condemnation to members of their own congregation. In addition to the LGBT people sitting in the congregation, many straight people have gay and lesbian family, friends, and co-workers.

If the traditional church thinks of itself as an agent of healing, then it must be clear to potential "patients" that the hospital is safe. Loving our LGBT brothers and sisters will require a moratorium on jokes about queers, along with sermons and teachings that discourage bullying and encourage models of faithful celibacy among gay Christians, such as Henri Nouwen. It may also mean advocating, as Tony Campolo has, that everyone have access to civil unions to ensure equal rights for all.[7]

Along with this, the church should be clear that though their traditional interpretation might be that homosexual behavior is a sin, homosexuality is not in a special category of "badness" all its own. When I was attending Bible college, I sometimes saw graffiti on bathroom walls that said, "Bob is a fag!" I

---

6. Estimates concerning the percent of LGBT people are politicized and vary widely. The National Bureau of Economic Research, "Size of the LGBT," claims that about 20 percent of the population is attracted to the same sex when studies use a "veiled elicitation method." On the other hand, in response to the question, "Do you, personally, identify as lesbian, gay, bisexual, or transgender?" asked by Gallup pollsters, only 3.4 percent of US adults responded affirmatively. See Gallup, "Special Report."

7. Campolo, "Possible Compromise."

was tempted to write underneath it, "Bill is greedy!" But I wasn't sure anyone would get the joke.

The 1 Corinthian passage that says "homosexual offenders" will not inherit the kingdom of God also says the greedy will not inherit the kingdom of God (6:9–10). While there is some question as to the exact definition of "homosexual offender," the definition of "greedy" is pretty clear: taking more than one's fair share. If every person on earth lived the average lifestyle of a North American, it would take four planets to sustain us.[8] In this light, most of us in the West fall into the category of greedy.

The conservative church has often communicated to gays and lesbians, "You are in a special category. You are the worst sinner here." What if the church were to communicate: "You are predisposed to sin like the rest of us. We recognize that you are here among us, and you are loved."

Two: Distinguish Between Orientation and Behavior

Within the traditional church, there is sometimes not a distinction between having a homosexual orientation and homosexual behavior. In high school, as I heard Christians talk with disdain about "homos," I always took it personally even though I wasn't having sex with anyone.

There is increasing evidence that certain people have a strong physiological predisposition toward homosexuality.[9] This doesn't necessarily mean it is okay to act on the predisposition, as there is evidence that some people have a predisposition toward alcoholism. However, we don't look down on alcoholics for merely *having the predisposition*. In fact, who do we respect more? The person who is not tempted to drink and never drinks—or the person who is strongly tempted to drink and yet resists the temptation?

To extend the analogy, Alcoholics Anonymous requires each person to own his or her temptation to drink. To deny being an alcoholic sets one up for drinking because the person isn't telling the truth and so cannot take the steps needed to stay sober. Similarly, if someone admits he or she is tempted toward homosexual acts, such truth-telling can help that person take steps to *not* act on the temptation.[10]

8. "Daily Infographic."

9. See for instance, Wade, "Pas de Deux."

10. I am using this analogy for the sake of arguing the traditionalist view, though I don't necessarily think alcoholism is analogous to homosexuality. Is homosexuality like having a temptation to drink alcohol excessively, or is it like being left-handed?

Three: Think Carefully about Identity Labels

I am sympathetic to the push-back from some of my evangelical friends that using the word "gay" in relation to myself is unhelpful. Conservative Christians rightly point out that our core identity is not defined by our sexuality, for we are not, as Freud argued, mostly a libido.

Yet Freud did come close to the important truth that at our deepest core, we are lovers, wanters, yearners.[11] As Psalm 130:6 puts it, "My soul *is* for the Lord, more than those watching for morning, watching for morning!"[12] Our core, our soul, is meant to love God and to be loved by God. To express our deepest identity, we might say we are "God-lovers," or "Beloved of God," or, imitating the person who best lived into those identities, we are Christ followers.

At the very least, if I describe myself as gay, I need to say I'm a gay Christian—where Christian is the noun and gay is the adjective. But to follow the logic of the conservative argument, why would I use a word to describe myself that refers to a sinful predisposition?

First, because it is the truth. Growing up in a traditionalist church, I became a shockingly good liar. Because I thought that being a homosexual was terrible, I learned to lie to myself and others. I pretended I didn't feel attraction and love for other guys and feigned interest in women. As a liar, part of my repentance is to tell the truth. I'm attracted to guys. In North America, the word for that is "gay."

Secondly, the word *gay* names a pattern of dispositions that are not *entirely* sinful. I'm fascinated by the report that homosexuality is common among male pianists and organists, yet almost entirely unknown in violinists.[13] Surely an orientation towards organ music is not wrong, nor is the fact many gay men prefer cooking to sports. Accepting myself as "gay" helps me understand the patterns that combine to make me who I am, even though aspects of that may go against what our culture sees as stereotypically masculine.

In the online community the Gay Christian Network (GCN) a minority of the members describe themselves as "Side B." ("Side A" refers to those who take the affirming position.) Side B gay Christians know themselves to be gay, but believe they should be celibate. By identifying themselves that way, they can support each other, befriend one another, and alert each other to resources for living a celibate life. They witness to the goodness of a celibate

---

11. See Smith, *Desiring the Kingdom*, on this point.

12. Young's Literal Translation (public domain).

13. Nobile, "Meaning of Gay," 38.

life to the majority of GCN members who believe that God affirms same-sex relationships.

While I'm making the case that to call oneself "gay" or "lesbian" is not necessarily wrong, I also believe it may not be helpful for everyone. In his excellent book, *A Bigger World Yet*, Tim Timmerman, a talented artist and professor, identifies himself not as "gay," but rather as having "high same-sex needs." He believes "homosexuality" is a modern idea that sexualizes our natural need for same-sex friendships. Tim's journey of faith is one of developing healthy non-sexual relationships with other men and of realizing the love of his heavenly father. Tim believes that to identify himself as "gay" would be untruthful and would get in the way of the friendships he wants to build with other men.

Other Christians use the term "same-sex attracted." Although they admit to a sexual and romantic attraction to people of the same-sex, they believe God intends them to stay single or marry the opposite sex. For them, identifying as "gay" or "lesbian" buys into corrupt notions of identity. Such Christians are trying to attend to the identity God gives them, rather than the identity our culture gives.[14]

Instead of focusing on identity labels, churches should ask a simple question of their members: "What does God seem to be doing in this person's life?" Rather than trying to use the "right" label, churches might shift their focus to having faith that God is at work in everyone. Churches can communicate this hope by asking, "What do you think God might be up to in this?" with genuine curiosity. Churches can encourage each person to welcome the work God is doing in his or her life and to pursue godly counsel.[15] As each person seeks this, amidst the company of a loving community of Christ-followers, the words that most accurately describe what God is doing in and through this person will become clear.

Four: Celebrate Celibacy

The night before I took a public vow of celibacy, I went out with some friends to a popular restaurant. Next to us, a group of frat boys kept making outrageous

14. Incidentally, in the gay community, it is becoming increasingly common not to label oneself at all. As the alphabet soup acronym LGBTTQQIAPPS (Lesbian, Gay, Bisexual, Transgender, Transsexual, Queer, Questioning, Intersex, Asexual, Pansexual, Polyamorous, Straight) continues to expand, it is obvious that human sexuality is difficult to categorize precisely.

15. By this, I mean counsel by someone who is interested in what the Spirit is up to rather than someone with an ideological ax to grind.

and loud toasts, and for the fun of it, we would raise our glasses with them. Not to be outdone, my gregarious friend Michael Munk raised his glass and bellowed, "To celibacy!" Glasses were raised at both tables—and then the whispered confusion began at the frat table. "To what? What did he say?"

This is the kind of odd witness the church ought to have. The most helpful thing traditionalist churches can do for LGBT members is to recapture a positive vision for celibacy.

For churches that stress their commitment to Scripture, the scriptural witness on celibacy is clear. Both Jesus and the Apostle Paul were single. Paul, writing in 1 Corinthians, advises singles to "remain unmarried as I am" (7:8). He later explains the unmarried person has more time to be concerned with "the affairs of the Lord, how to please the Lord" (7:32). Because of this, Paul believes the person who marries "does well; and he who refrains from marriage will do better" (7:38). Yet the idea of celibacy as a special "gift" is sometimes used to undermine this call—for it is a "gift" few people want and a "gift" even fewer claim to have.

But as Albert Hsu helpfully points out in his book *Singles at the Crossroads*, Paul is not referring to a special celibacy superpower given by the Holy Spirit. Rather he is using "gift" here in its most basic sense.[16] Notice Paul's wording: "each has a particular gift from God, one having one kind [given the context: singleness] and another a different kind [given the context: marriage]" (7:7).

This coheres well with the witness of the church through the centuries. Both marriage and singleness are important for the life of the church, and each involve difficulties that can become potential avenues for training in holiness.

In our mobile, individualistic culture marriage is the one place where we can imagine ongoing intimacy and mutual support. Given our increasingly autonomous and disconnected culture, in which people feel increasingly lonely, romantic love promises a kind of salvation. Thus for a single person, it requires faith to believe that singleness might be God's good gift.

But in the context of the kingdom, and specifically the church, we are given "brothers and sisters, mothers and children" (Mark 10:30). The church is to be a kind of family that loves single people and asks for their love in return. The church needs the time, energy, and talents of single people—and single people need both the love and the demands of the church.

As a celibate single, I sometimes find myself seduced by Hollywood's stories of salvation through romantic love. I'm tempted to question God's

---

16. Hsu, *Singles*, 48.

goodness and adopt what Paige Benton Brown jokingly refers to as her life verse, "If any man would come after me, let him."[17]

But day by day, as I participate in a church with a robust body life that highly values single people, I find myself touched, hugged, encouraged, loved, challenged, humbled, sinned against, and known. I must confess my life is good and then gratefully go on.

Changing church culture so that singles are valued and integrated into congregational life requires a lot of work. Singles themselves won't always have the vision for this work and will sometimes be self-absorbed and busy. To change the culture in any given church will require ongoing teaching and honest conversations.

It isn't enough, however, for the conservative church to send LGBT people to the basement on Thursday nights to learn about "sexual wholeness," thinking that by offering "right teaching" they are loving gays. The church needs to identify these members of the congregation as family so they can better imagine living a single life as a "gift" from God.

My friend Heather comments that Christians need to "have some respect for the difficulty of celibacy as a chosen life and for the spiritual work and potential spiritual growth it involves. It's a big thing to be asking of someone, and people who embark on it deserve our respect as well as support, not our disdain or uneasiness for being gay in the first place."[18]

Five: Support of Heterosexual Marriage for LGBT People

Conservative churches should truly endeavor to value their single members, because most LGBT folks in such churches will end up being single. But for some LGBT people, staying in a traditionalist church might mean marrying someone of the opposite sex.

Just three years ago I was against the marriage of gays and lesbians to opposite-sex partners. Given all the difficulties of marriage, I felt that adding the issue of sexual orientation would not be wise, but my view has changed.

A good friend of mine, who at one time lived with a gay lover, has married a woman, and after five years of marriage, he is honestly happy—and his wife feels the same way. My friend attributes the success of his marriage to the support of his tightly knit church community.

17. Brown, "Singled Out."
18. Personal email.

Another highly publicized example is the marriage of Josh and Laurel "Lolly" Weed. After ten years of marriage and three kids, Josh came out as gay on his blog. He was subsequently interviewed by numerous news agencies. I was fairly skeptical about this story until I checked out his blog, where he writes sensibly and wisely:

> Sex is about more than just visual attraction and lust and it is about more than just passion and infatuation. . . . Basically when sex is done right, at its deepest level it is about intimacy. It is about one human being connecting with another human being they love. It is a beautiful physical manifestation of two people being connected in a truly vulnerable, intimate manner because they love each other profoundly. It is bodies connecting and souls connecting. It is beautiful and rich and fulfilling and spiritual and amazing. Many people never get to this point in their sex lives because it requires incredible communication, trust, vulnerability, and connection.[19]

Josh makes a convincing case that sexual desire is a secondary matter in loving someone well. To a lesser or greater degree, most every marriage struggles with issues of sexual desire—and Josh's marriage has particular challenges in that regard. But given all the goods of marriage and the committed love that Josh and Lolly have toward each other, a good marriage is still possible for them.

Lolly writes, "I knew that we had the kind of relationship that could work through hard trials and circumstances. I had faith in him and I had faith in our love. I did not choose to marry someone who is gay. I chose to marry Josh Weed, the man that I love, and to accept all of him. I have never regretted it."[20] Josh and Lolly have been able to journey into deeper trust, vulnerability, and communication through the difficulties of their marriage in part because of the substantial support they receive from their Mormon church.

Yet I have also seen the extreme heartache of men and women who entered unknowingly into such marriages and ended up feeling unloved in spite of their best efforts. Thus *it is crucial that any same-sex attracted person be honest with a potential opposite-sex partner about his or her orientation before getting married.* Such marriages should be entered into with caution, counseling from trusted sources, and have a wide support network.

In our sex-obsessed age, such marriages might seem like a miracle—perhaps even more of a miracle than the marriages of homosexuals who were "fixed" or "cured." But such "miracles" are possible in the context of supportive church bodies, where they can become positive witnesses of the power of committed, mature, self-sacrificing love.

19. Weed, "Club Unicorn," para 17.
20. Ibid., question 6, para 10.

Conclusion

According to research done by the Barna Group of young adults aged sixteen to twenty-nine, 91 percent said the word "anti-homosexual" best describes Christianity, as did 80 percent of young churchgoers.[21] Though Christ was a friend of tax collectors and sinners, the church hasn't followed his example.

Realizing this, we now have an opportunity.

If the church is going to ask others to repent of a "sinful lifestyle," then it will need to model its own repentance. Growing up gay in the church, I experienced the church's condemnation and judgment—something Jesus rebuked far more than homosexuality![22]

For the church to repent, members will need to learn practices such as: owning past and current prejudice against gays and lesbians, taking responsibility for past and current behaviors, and having the humility to confess. Confession is a healing act that transcends our personal stories. That is, my act of confession invites others to confess.

By contrast, denouncing the sin of others creates silence, resentment, and misunderstanding. Acts of confession might enable gays and lesbians to hear the message of the conservative church.

While such an idea might appear idealistic and impractical, there are Christians who have found ways to do this. Donald Miller, in his book *Blue Like Jazz*, tells how he and his friends built a "Confession Booth" on their college campus during a party weekend. When students ventured into the booth, Miller and friends confessed the sins of Christianity to surprised students.[23]

Andrew Marin, author of *Love is an Orientation*, has organized "We're Sorry" campaigns gathering Christians to attend LGBT pride parades. Rather than hurling the usual "Christian" condemnation at participants, Marin and friends hold signs that say, "I'm sorry Christians judge you," and "I'm sorry for the way churches have treated you." Marin and others movingly describe the response of tears, hugs, and forgiveness they receive.[24]

Jamie Arpin-Ricc participated in a "We're Sorry" campaign at a Pride Parade and shared a moving letter he received in response:

> I read your signs and was hit by tremendous emotion and was moved to tears at the reality of it as I marched by . . .

---

21. Kinnaman and Lyons, *UnChristian*, 27.

22. An admittedly easy computation, since Jesus didn't explicitly mention homosexuality even once.

23. Miller, *Blue Like Jazz*, 116ff.

24. See for instance, Albert, "I hugged."

I somehow felt a touch of the weight of all that we as humans do to each other that is hurtful—and the importance of doing something positive about it, regardless of who we are and where we stand on any issue.

The power of an apology is amazing and even though I don't think I have met any of you personally, your presence and willingness to apologize for a history that you have inherited was truly appreciated.[25]

The debate over homosexuality provides the conservative church with the opportunity to model one of the most fundamental of Christian practices: repentance. In doing so it might invite others to do the same.

Beyond that, the debate about homosexuality invites the church to press into practices that will build up the entire church, such as the recollection that churches are not "museums for saints but hospitals for sinners," telling the truth about what God is doing in relation to our sexuality rather than what we think God should do, inviting singles into full participation in the Christian family, including LGBT members, and forming a robust community that supports marriages undergoing all kinds of challenges—including the lack of sexual desire for the other.

As I've tried to suggest in the earlier chapters of this book, suffering LGBT folk are a sign that something is wrong with our vision of church. We need to live into being family together in more intense, committed ways than we've yet imagined. As we do so, we'll find that we have a healing hand to offer gays, lesbians, and all who are hurting. Connected to the head, which is Christ, and to each other as members, we may find ourselves loving others as Christ.

Questions for Discussion

1. Regardless of your stance on same-sex relationships, what can you appreciate about the traditionalist view?

2. How might being family to LGBT members in your midst be an important practice for your church?

3. How can your church repent for the ways it has treated LGBT folk or others?

25. Kampen, "I'm Sorry."

14

A Committed Affirmation

"Our age is in a crisis
—not so much of homosexuality—
but more generally of erotic faithfulness."

—Sarah Coakley

At age twenty-three, shortly after moving to San Francisco, I began attending affirming churches as a way of learning about what it means to be gay.[1] Having grown up in a fairly pietistic church, I was glad to worship with people who understood the "social gospel."

In high school, when I was honest with myself, the "good news" didn't always seem so good. As I tried to evangelize my friends, the gospel seemed to boil down to, "Please have a relationship with my invisible friend Jesus." When my friends asked me what a relationship with Jesus meant, I would fumble, "Well, it means having daily devotional times. Then you've got to go to church on Sunday for worship. And you've got to give up drinking and sex."

My career as an evangelist left a lot to be desired. But in San Francisco I experienced joy as I learned from liberal, affirming churches that the gospel not only includes the soul, but the body. Liberal writers and theologians helped me understand that Jesus cared not only about piety, but about politics, economics, and social structures. These writers helped me love the Old

---

1. Although I was living at Sojourners, we had our Sunday gathering at night, which freed me to attend other churches in the morning.

Testament as I began to see the prophets' passionate appeals for justice and peace.[2] The liberal church challenged me to meet Jesus in the poor just as much as in my prayer closet.

When I began working as an RN on the AIDS ward at San Francisco General Hospital, I saw the liberal church organizing to increase funding for AIDS research and advance civil rights for gays and lesbians. If the Reverend Martin Luther King Jr. was a "drum major for justice," then here were folks attempting to be the band.

But though I resonated with the way liberal churches were taking on my deepest social passions at the time, I also began to wonder if they were only seeing half of Jesus' message. Most of my AIDS patients had averaged over 1,000 sexual partners, and I understood how much of that behavior was prompted by oppression. Suffering from social rejection and self-loathing, many gay men were seeking solace in sex.

I knew the best response to those who were living in oppression was love and grace, over and over again, but as I read the Gospels, I didn't see Jesus patronizing those who were oppressed. Rather, in Jesus' exchange with the woman caught in adultery, he asks if anyone condemns her, and she responds, "No one sir." Then Jesus replies, "Neither do I condemn you. Go your way, and from now on do not sin again" (John 8:11), liberating her from self-righteous judgment, while exhorting her to stop sinning.

We are all, in the words of my friend Eric, "victimizing victims," and Jesus challenges us with both love and truth (indeed, part of his love is telling us the truth). In the words of W. H. Auden, a gay Christian poet, "I believe because he fulfills none of my dreams, because he is in every respect the opposite of what he would be if I could have made him in my own image." Auden speaks of how Jesus causes "all sides of my being to cry 'Crucify him!'"[3]

While my sexual desires tempted me to adopt a permissive sexual ethic, I also saw the loneliness, self-absorption, and alienation of this way of life in my patients. Given my own history of pain and my temptation to medicate pain with sex, I knew I would need a band of brothers and sisters to help me resist sexual libertinism—and I realized I wouldn't find that in most mainline Protestant churches.

In this chapter I want to challenge the permissive sexual ethic that characterizes many progressive churches while making it clear that affirming churches might be right in blessing same-sex relationships.

2. Jack Bernard, Steve Reed, (from Sojourners) and David Poppinga turned me on to liberationist writers and theologians.

3. Auden, "Purely Subjective," 184–97.

How the Affirming Church is Reading Scripture with Integrity

In chapter 10, "Walking Humbly with God," I discussed why the usual "clobber passages" in the Bible may be directed at the wrong people. Though those passages inform much of the debate on homosexuality in the church, perhaps we are missing the most relevant passage of all: Acts 10–15.

In Acts 10:9–16, Peter has a vision of food that is forbidden to Jews. Three times he hears a voice saying, "Do not call anything impure that God has made clean" (Acts 10:15b, NIV). The story goes on to make clear that God is not just graciously expanding Peter's culinary palate, for Peter later interprets the vision as follows: "You yourselves know that it is unlawful for a Jew to associate with or to visit a Gentile; but God has shown me that I should not call anyone profane or unclean" (Acts 10:28b).

The Greek words translated as "profane" and "unclean" had to do with the priestly (Levitical) laws concerning purity. These words might also be translated as "defiled," "unholy," and "foul."

Baptist theologian James McClendon writes that just as Peter quotes from the Hebrew Scriptures that "I shall pour out my Spirit on all humanity" (Acts 2:17), and asserts that *this is that* which was spoken by the prophet Joel" (2:16), the task of good Bible interpretation is to recognize when "this *is* that."[4] Given our modern context, we need to notice when we find ourselves in situations similar to those narrated in the Bible and notice "this is that."

Applying this interpretive wisdom, we need to ask the question, who are the people we think of as "profane and unclean?" Historically, this has applied to people of different races, as conveyed by racial slurs such as "wetback," "chink," and so on, which connote "profane and unclean." While we still have a very long way to go—and few of us readily admit the great distance we still have to travel—the church as a whole has acknowledged the problem of racism in our society and, in some quarters, is actively repenting of this sin.

Words such as, "queer," "faggot," and "homo" conveyed to me the message that I was defiled, unclean, and foul. Perhaps LGBT folk are to some Christians what ancient Gentiles were to Jews.

When I was attending school to become a registered nurse, I came across an interesting article that attempted to explain why nurses have traditionally worn white uniforms. The author made the claim that "impurity" is often associated with what bodily orifices spew forth. So nurses, working in the context of what all the orifices spew, wear white to symbolically say, "We're not contaminated; we're clean!"

4. McClendon, *Ethics*, 32.

I found this provocative as I thought about the Levitical laws, which identify ejaculation and menstruation as unclean. For ancient people, perhaps homosexuality (among other things) represented a confusion about the proper "ins and outs" of orifices.

We no longer go through rites of purification after ejaculating or menstruating, for we realize that spiritual health is not about what goes in or out of orifices, but what comes out of the heart. Jesus taught us this when he said, "It's not what goes into your mouth that defiles you; you are defiled by the words that come out of your mouth" (Matt 15:11, NLT). So perhaps it is not the "faggot" who is defiled, but rather the one who says "faggot," or similar slurs, with the intent to harm.

For the believers in Acts, the ultimate question was not whether Gentiles could become Christians, as for centuries Gentiles had converted to Judaism by being circumcised and adopting the Jewish laws. The question for them was, could Gentiles become Christians as Gentiles? Could Gentiles become Christians and *not* be circumcised? Could Gentiles become Christians without observing Torah? Thankfully, for most of us, the final answer was—and is—"yes!"

For the believers in Acts, the Jew-Gentile question was eventually decided by the fact that they saw the Spirit at work in uncircumcised, non-Torah observing Gentiles. Peter stands up in the Jerusalem counsel and preaches, "God, who knows the human heart, testified to them by giving them the Holy Spirit, just as he did to us" (Acts 15:8). How might we know if the Holy Spirit is at work in gay and lesbian couples today? Can LGBT folk join God's people without "cutting off" their sexuality by following a Levitical code that prohibits a man from lying with a man—a code that many of their straight brothers and sisters do not follow in other ways?

Nurturing Fellowship: Testifying to the Spirit's Work

Stephen Fowl, in his book *Engaging Scripture*, points out it wasn't the responsibility of the Gentiles to testify on their own behalf. Rather, respected members of the community who were themselves clearly filled with the Spirit testified that the Spirit had been poured out on the Gentiles. Fowl wonders if we have the type of deep relationships that might allow us to see the work of the Spirit in each other's lives. He writes:

> Spirit experience, in both the New Testament and the present, is not self-interpreting. It is often quite difficult to read the Spirit. As I have already indicated, as related in Acts, the very manner in

which the Gentiles were included as full members of the people of God presupposes a whole set of ecclesiological [church] practices which are largely absent from Christianity in the US. Most churches do not train and nurture people in forming the sorts of friendships out of which testimony about the Spirit's work might arise.[5]

Some years ago, a friend of mine gave me a picture of him and his beautiful wife posing arm-in-arm in front of the San Francisco skyline—a romantic picture that I happily pinned above my desk. Recently, due to their divorce, I took it down, reflecting that one had to know them intimately to realize the pain involved in their seemingly picture-perfect relationship.

The affirming church is in a unique position to answer the question about whether or not the Spirit has been poured out in same-sex relationships. Does the Spirit seem to animate same-sex couples in self-giving love, hospitality, joy, and generosity? Do such relationships seem to build up both the individuals involved and the surrounding community?[6] The answer must not be a glib "of course!" for the sake of political correctness and self-righteousness in the face of traditionalist Christians, but must be borne out of close friendships with same-sex couples.

Breaking Fellowship:
The Church's First and Deepest Wound

Although the believers in Acts decisively welcomed Gentiles *as* Gentiles into the church, the Jerusalem Council did require Gentiles to adopt some specific practices. The council asked Gentiles to "abstain from what has been sacrificed to idols and from blood and from what is strangled and from fornication" (Acts 15:29b).

In retrospect, this seems like an odd list. We might cynically see it as a list of the negotiated concessions to the hardliners in order to get agreement to a radical proposal. But commentators tell us something important was going on. Central to the life of the early believers was table fellowship and communion. By asking the Gentiles to refrain from foods prohibited by Torah, church leaders were seeking to preserve fellowship between the two groups. If Gentiles abstained from food with blood in it, or food that had been sacrificed or strangled, Jews could eat with them. Moreover, church leaders were also

---

5. Fowl, *Engaging Scripture*, 125.

6. Obviously, the standard for gay couples can't be *higher* than for straight couples.

addressing the common Jewish stereotype that Gentiles were idolatrous and sexually immoral, thus further reconciling the two factions.

In the decades that followed, the church became primarily a Gentile church. In spite of the fact that we Gentiles were grafted into the deep root of Judaism, from which we received the faith, we took over. Theologian John Howard Yoder identifies this as Christianity's first and deepest wound.[7] For through it, the church lost its witness of the reconciliation through Christ of Jew and Gentile, one of the most basic polarities in ancient world. In the centuries that followed, the Christian persecution of Jews became one of the most horrific signs of unfaithfulness and the dissolution of the union we once shared in Christ.

It is impossible to recreate exactly what happened in those tumultuous early years of Christianity, but there is some evidence that the Gentiles became arrogant.[8] Perhaps, in the name of liberty from the law, Gentiles stopped being sensitive to their Jewish brothers and sisters. Perhaps, in the name of freedom, they ate whatever they wanted, forgetting that unity requires sacrifice.

Perhaps something similar is happening today. In June 2012, *Christian Century* reported that over the preceding ten years, the majority of Americans switched from thinking that homosexuality is "morally wrong" (53 percent) to thinking that it is "morally acceptable" (54 percent).[9] The affirming side is gaining adherents and may ultimately show itself to be on "the right side of history."

Yet affirming Christians may be cutting themselves off from their traditionalist brothers and sisters—and also from their historic Christian roots. The permissive sexual ethic that tends to accompany the affirming position undermines relationships (of both gays and straights), subverts community, and weakens our capacity to live in covenant with God and one another.

Recovering Jesus' Revolutionary Vision: The Church

Diana Butler Bass contends that mainline Protestantism, in the face of membership decline, has wrestled well with the question of what Christianity might look like in the twenty-first century. These churches have placed Jesus' great commandment, "Love the Lord with all your heart, soul, and mind, and your neighbor as yourself," at the core of faith. She writes that liberal Christianity is

---

7. See Yoder, *Jewish-Christian Schism Revisited.*

8. See, for instance, Paul's treatment of food sacrificed to idols in Romans 14–15.

9. "New Normal," 9.

a form of faith that cares for one's neighbor, the common good, and fosters equality, but is, at the same time, a transformative personal faith that is warm, experiential, generous, and thoughtful. This new expression of Christianity maintains the historic liberal passion for serving others but embraces Jesus' injunction that a vibrant love for God is the basis for a meaningful life. These Christians link spirituality with social justice as a path of peace and biblical faith.[10]

I find her vision compelling, and I know LGBT Christians who are finding a welcoming home in historic mainline denominations. Yet FIRE (the commitment to freedom, individualism, rights, and equality I describe in chapter 11) can work against the core commitment of loving God and one's neighbor as one's self.

Catholic writer Ross Douthat expresses this concern in a response to Bass's essay, arguing that the individualism of the mainline church

has consequences that liberal Christians as well more traditional believers should find more worrying than cheering: Consequences for local community (because it's harder to care for your neighbor when you don't have a congregation around you to provide resources and support), consequences for society as a whole (because the declining institutional churches leaves a void that our insolvent government is unlikely to effectively fill, no matter how many elections the Democratic Party wins), and consequences for private morality (because an individualistic faith is more likely to encourage solipsism and narcissism, in which the voice of the ego is mistaken for the voice of the divine).

The title of Bass' book, *Christianity After Religion: The End of Church and a New Spiritual Awakening,* conveys Bass's assumption that new forms of community will appear that better express the Christian vision than the institutional church. Douthat sharply challenges this notion:

Like many religious progressives, Bass has great hopes for Christianity after organized religion, Christianity after the institutional church. But I feel like we already know what that Christianity looks like: It's the self-satisfied, self-regarding, all-too-American faith that Christian Smith and others have encountered when they survey today's teenagers and young adults, which conceives of God as part divine butler, part cosmic therapist, and which jettisons the more challenging aspects of Christianity that the traditional

10. Bass, "Can Christianity," para 9.

churches and denominations, for all their many sins and follies, at
least tried to hand down to us intact.[11]

Perhaps Douthat's critique is overly harsh, but it names a troubling tendency
in our consumer culture. Decades ago Robert Bellah, et al., in the prescient
book *Habits of the Heart*, described how we were losing the words, the vo-
cabulary itself, to talk about the practices of committing to one another. The
authors of *Habits* describe how we are losing our ability to form thick communities (communities of deep, committed relationship) by exchanging these
for thin groups (affinity groups that rely on superficial characteristics to bond
people together). Whether it is an Airstream trailer club, a collection of Facebook friends, or a moms' group, we're unlikely to "lay down our lives" for one
another when our relationships are so thin and commitment free.

As Bass envisions it, the new post-institutional church can take place
in "neighborhoods, community gardens, city streets, public transit, parks,
cafés, and coffee shops; galleries, museums, and libraries; festivals, fairs, and
farmer's markets; rallies and debates; public schools, congregations, and social
networks."[12] But Jesus calls us to participate in the creation of a new social,
political, economic, spiritual reality called "church." To propose that the Jesus
revolution can base itself in something other than church is to miss the passion and point of the New Testament.

Because I, like Bass, have concerns about the institutional church, I've
gravitated towards a much smaller and radically relational congregation modeled on the fellowship gatherings of the early church.[13]

Recovering a Committed, Self-Sacrificing Love Ethic

We can define "church" as a group of people dedicated to the way of love modeled by Jesus. As 1 John 3:16 says, "We know love by this, that he laid down
his life for us—and we ought to lay down our lives for one another." In the
Christian vision, love is not just random acts of kindness, a disposition to be
nice, or warm and affectionate feelings toward others. Love is defined by the
committed, self-sacrificing life of Jesus.

This committed, self-sacrificing life has to do with how we relate to God
(giving up attractive idols in order to do God's will) and how we relate to
others (enduring significant pain in order to care for others). While such a
lifestyle may seem daunting, this is what we were designed for as humans. As

11. Douthat, "Liberal Christianity," last para.

12. Bass, *Christianity after Religion*, 263.

13. Which, to be honest, does not escape all the hazards of institutions.

we devote our lives to this calling, we live out the purposes for which we were made, and our lives become more abundant.

Regarding the conflict within the church about homosexuality, the most significant thing the affirming church can do for gays and lesbians *is to recover and celebrate a love ethic that emphasizes faithfulness and commitment in the context of a robust church community.* Recovering a love ethic that celebrates fidelity, commitment, and community will not only bless gays and lesbians, but it will also encourage dialogue with traditionalists and will ensure the vitality of the affirming church.

As theologian Sarah Coakley writes of the demanding task before the church:

> The re-thinking of celibacy and faithful vowed relations (whether heterosexual or homosexual) in an age of instantly commodified desire and massive infidelity is a task of daunting proportions, of which no-one can be very confident of wide-spread success.
>
> But as Gregory [of Nyssa] himself warns, we cannot believe it unless we see it lived. He writes, "Any theory divorced from living examples . . . is like an unbreathing statue." And there, perhaps, lies the true challenge for us today: the counter-cultural production— not of film-stars, sports heroes or faithless royal families—but of erotic "saints" to inspire us.[14]

If gays and lesbians grow up thinking, "if anyone knew who I really was, they wouldn't love me," then one of the most healing experiences would be the gift of giving and receiving unconditional love in the context of a gay union or marriage.

But such relationships are not the norm. While gay culture offers "affirmation," it does not teach the practices of forgiveness, patience, humility, listening, and self-giving that make committed relationships of fidelity possible. But gays and lesbians might look to churches to honor their commitment and love by teaching such practices within the context of their community life.

As Andrew Sullivan writes:

> It is not simply about "taming" or "civilizing" gay men. It is also the deepest means for the liberation of homosexuals, providing them with the only avenue for sexual and emotional development that can integrate them as equal human beings and remove from them the hideous historic option of choosing between their joy and

14. Coakley, "Best," para 7 and 8.

their dignity. It is about deepening and widening and strengthening the possibility of true intimacy between two human beings.[15]

To paraphrase an old saying, the cultivation of such relationships takes a village. Many heterosexual relationships are floundering, yet gay relationships have even less social support. As Jeffrey John notes, a church congregation can encourage members to offer "simple things that married couples take for granted—joint invitations, anniversary cards, inquiries about one's partner . . . immensely important signs of affirmation."[16] Churches can raise up mentors who have learned the practice of faithful love to journey with newly married or committed gay couples. Such mentors can demonstrate care by asking hard questions and challenging couples to walk the difficult road of fidelity. In this way, churches can encourage gay relationships to grow and flourish, bearing witness to fidelity, love, and community amidst our destructive consumer culture.

Thus gay relationships are not just a way of happiness for two people who happen to be in love, but signs that all kinds of people (gay, straight, transgender, etc.) can be brought together in love within the revolutionary context of the church. Jeffrey John writes:

> The church understands marriage as a covenant within which two people are called to find their truest selves by giving themselves away in love to one another. It is a "mystery" or sacrament of God because it potentially reflects the mystery of self-giving love which is at the heart of the Trinity, the dynamic, creative interchange of love which binds persons in one, yet such that they become more fully themselves. At the same time, the couple are a cell in the Body of Christ, the Church, where we are all learning, often painfully and sacrificially, to live in love with each other, to understand and enter into the experience of each other, so as to model and reflect at the level of our common life the unity-in-diversity which is the life of God.[17]

As we connect our lives with others who are different from ourselves through the committed, sacrificial love of Jesus, we live the joyful, holy, welcoming dance of the Trinity in the midst of our broken world. I cannot imagine anything more beautiful, more healing, more attractive, or more affirming. This dance not only includes quirky queers, but also liberals and conservatives. In

---

15. John, "*Permanent, Faithful,*" 52, quoting Sullivan, *Love Undetectable*, 67.

16. Ibid., 50.

17. Ibid., 52.

the next chapter, I'll suggest some steps we might learn to make such a broader inclusion possible.

Questions for Discussion

1. Regardless of your stance on same-sex relationships, what arguments from the affirming church do you find most helpful?

2. Christian love is committed and faithful. To what extent do you see that lived out in your church?

3. How can your church be more supportive of all the marriages in its midst?

15

"May All Be One"

"Far from making me feel different and special,
my [spiritual] experiences made me feel
the same, ordinary, and interconnected."

—Julia Cameron

Pastor Brian McLaren, estimating that LGBT folk make up approximately 6 percent of the population, writes, "If each gay person has two parents, the issue affects 18 percent of the population. If each gay person has one sibling and one friend, we're up to 30 percent who are directly affected by the issue."[1] Because so many people are directly affected, and because attitudes about homosexuality are changing in North America, many local congregations are struggling with conflict over homosexuality.

That conflict can become very personal, even if those wrestling with the issue are not gay themselves. "My pastor just married a gay couple. Denominational leaders are upset. Do I stand with her against them?" Or, "I love family members who are gay and lesbian. The pastor of my church preaches about how we should support laws that keep gays and lesbians from marrying. Do I leave my church in protest?"

In the midst of conflict, rather than pushing for our side to "win," we would do well to remember Christ's fervent prayer for Christians as he faced his execution: "that they may become completely one, so that the world may know that you have sent me" (John 17:23). As followers of Jesus, who lost everything on the cross in order to bring about a greater good, we would do well

1. McLaren, "Farewell," para 11.

to pause and reframe the conflict. Rather than worsening the church's disunity by trying to "win" the battle, we might work together towards deeper unity by humbly listening for the Spirit's guidance through this conflict. One way to journey towards deeper Spirit-led unity is to ask questions about how God might be forming us through the conflict. Some guiding questions, which we will return to at the end of this chapter, might be:

> How is God at work in this conflict? How can we cooperate in the midst of this conflict?

> What might we learn from this conflict about church unity and being one in Christ?

> How can we work to make Jesus' Gethsemane prayer a reality?

Disputable Disputes

So much of the antagonism in this debate revolves around verses at the beginning of Romans. Perhaps the antidote for peace lies in the conclusion to Romans, specifically in Romans chapters 14–15.

Paul addresses questions concerning food and holy days. Some people eat only vegetables, while others eat everything. Some observe special days while others see all days as equal. We might see these as minor concerns: something like the modern disputes between vegetarians and carnivores, or arguments about whether Saturday or Sunday is a special day.

In the ancient world, however, Jews were known as a distinct people for three primary things: dietary laws (especially not eating pork), Sabbath observance, and circumcision. Jews had fought and died for these distinctives. On the other hand, Jews characterized Gentiles as those who engaged in idolatrous food and sexual practices. Theological perspectives on food and holy days were deeply felt by early Christians.

Paul begins by calling the Christians in Rome to welcome the "weak" in regard to these serious disagreements that Paul labels as "disputable matters" (14:1, NIV). Paul's concern is that they, even in important theological matters related to the law and idolatry, "Accept one another then, just as Christ has accepted you, in order to bring praise to God" (15:7, NIV)[2] and, that in whatever they do, that it be "from faith" (14:23).

---

2. Wright, "Romans," argues that this section (verses 7–13) "serves as the concluding paragraph for the major theological exposition not only of chaps. 12–15, but of the letter as a whole," 730.

Early in his argument Paul reveals his rationale for allowing such a diversity of opinion. "Who are you to pass judgment on servants of another? It is before their own lord that they stand or fall. And they will be upheld, for the Lord is able to make them stand" (14:4). Twice in chapter 14 Paul admonishes them not to "despise" (NRSV) or have "contempt" (NIV) for one another (3, 10). Four times in the chapter Paul urges the Christians to not judge one another (3, 4, 10, 13) for each person is accountable "before the judgment seat of God" (10).

The question confronts us: can the debate over same-sex relationships in the church be considered a "disputable matter"? Ken Wilson, a Vineyard Church pastor, I think rightly contends that the debate over homosexuality fits this category because:

> 1) it doesn't involve a matter of basic Christian dogma such as we find the great ecumenical creeds . . . 2) the debate brings two or more biblical truths into dynamic tension (e.g., mercy-judgment, law-grace, free will-predestination) so that both parties make reasonable appeals to Scripture . . . 3) faithful Christians take different views on the issue.[3]

In Essentials Unity

As my New Testament professor at Bible college encouraged us in response to the question of Christian unity: "In essentials unity, in non-essentials liberty, in all things, charity."[4] Despite my professor's fundamentalist bent, this is an excellent guideline.

The first two clauses, "In essentials unity, in non-essentials liberty," stand in tension with each other. "In non-essentials liberty" reminds us that we should not let all differences drive us apart. Christ reconciles us across gender, racial, and economic divisions. If we can't allow differences, then the power of our witness is diminished. A great witness we can offer the world is not that we agree on everything, but that people can hold very different opinions on important topics and still love and respect one another.

"In essentials unity" reminds us that if we differ about "essentials," we begin to lose the essence of our faith. The difficulty comes in distinguishing the "essential" from the "non-essential."

---

3. Wilson, *A Letter to My Congregation*, 107–8.

4. The phrase was not original to my professor. It is often attributed to Augustine, though church historians have shown that it originated with a seventeenth-century German Lutheran theologian named Rupertus Meldenius.

We first need the historical context for distinguishing essential from non-essential. Christians have identified the important teachings that differ from the essential, core Christian beliefs as "heresy." While the word has fallen out of common usage, it is a useful tool for distinguishing between essentials and non-essentials. This distinction is made by noticing what the biblical writers themselves saw as central (essential) and peripheral (non-essential).

First Corinthians 15:3–4 speaks of what is most important:

> For I handed on to you as of first importance what I in turn had received: that Christ died for our sins in accordance with the Scriptures, and that he was buried, and that he was raised on the third day in accordance with the Scriptures.

Notice the things of "first importance" are about the Christian story rather than about how one interprets the Bible's ethical teachings.

Theologian Steven Harmon, based on his study of the biblical teaching concerning heresy and division, makes the point that "A heretic is someone whose account of the Christian story is so dangerously inadequate that it's really an altogether different story than the biblical story of the Triune God."[5] Anyone who has read this far can see clearly that teaching about same-sex relationships (one way or the other) doesn't meet the definition of "heresy."

As I've tried to show in previous chapters, homosexuality is a relatively minor theme in Scripture, and good interpreters of Scripture can come to different views with integrity while remaining true to the core Christian story. Neither the affirming nor the traditionalist perspectives on homosexuality endanger "the biblical story of the Triune God."

Agreement on Unity

A central mystery of the Trinity is that three persons are one God. Although each person of the Trinity is different, together they dwell in such profound unity that they are one. Ironically, both the Christian left and right fundamentally agree that in God, difference is brought together into unity. The disagreement is over what makes for valid "difference."

The affirming church sees homosexual orientation as a reflection of the diversity or "difference" created by God. For the affirming church, welcoming gays as gays and including them in a diverse church is one way to witness to how God brings difference together into a unity.

5. Harmon, *Ecumenism*, 20–21.

The traditionalist church, on the other hand, sees sexual difference as the primary human division that is brought together in marriage to bear witness to the unifying nature of God. For traditionalists, to bring together two people of the same sex falls short of what marriage is meant to signify.[6]

For both sides, the goal of bringing difference together into unity is the same. Recognizing both sides of the debate are pointing to the biblical story of the Triune God may help conservatives and liberals have empathy for one another.

Underlying Concerns

If both conservatives and liberals agree that an essential aspect of the nature of God is revealed when difference is brought together into unity, then the energy and passion behind this debate stems from underlying concerns.

Imagine that over Thanksgiving dinner two brothers find themselves yelling at each other over whether or not to use the red tablecloth. For one brother, it might be about remembering their mom, who always used the red tablecloth. For the other, it might be that the red tablecloth reminds him too much of their mom's absence. As long as they keep shouting about the color of the cloth, they'll get nowhere. But if they manage to get past the heated emotions and talk about their underlying concerns, they'll grow to understand each other better.

Similarly, the underlying issues for Christians may be, "I think your approach undermines the authority of Scripture," or "I don't think you are taking seriously enough the need for justice," or "I think your position threatens my vision of family," or "I think your position ignores equality and rights." If the two sides can focus on their underlying concerns, they might be able to understand one another better, even if they don't end up agreeing. Thus they can agree to disagree without undermining the unity of Christ's church.

In Non-Essentials Liberty

If we are to exercise liberty and charity in the church, then it is crucial for church members to identify the debate over homosexuality as one that is a "non-essential" to the faith. This will not be an easy task because historically, Protestants have not instinctively exhibited tolerance in faith. Catholic

---

6. It would be interesting to apply this same logic to churches. Does a church of all white people constitute a church? Does a church of all middle-class people constitute a church?

theologian Rebem Alves notices that for Protestants, the notion of salvation by faith often means salvation through believing the "right" things.[7]

Any deviation from "believing the right things" becomes profoundly threatening to Protestants, as it might jeopardize one's salvation. Thus Protestant churches are prone to divide over relatively minor points of doctrine. The fact there are an estimated 33,000 different Protestant denominations bears out Alves's observation.[8]

The debate over homosexuality offers Protestants an opportunity to think well about the difference between essentials and non-essentials in Christian doctrine. If Protestants come to better clarity about what comprises the essentials of faith, then the debate over homosexuality might help avoid even deeper and more unnecessary divisions in the future.

Indeed, the ability to live in unity while having differences of opinion on important topics might be one of the signs that God is up to something and that the church is not just another affinity group of people who already look, act, and think alike.

Life Together: A Taste of the Kingdom

Practicing unity amidst real differences might seem like a nice ideal, but how can it be lived out? By releasing local congregations to decide non-essential issues, the debate over homosexuality might help us reclaim the early church vision of the *polis*: a gathering of different people seeking to order their relationships according to God's kingdom.

Ideally, figuring out how to live together will be practiced at a local level. In this respect, tending the church is like tending a garden. When I lived in Sacramento, I loved eating cherry tomatoes fresh off the vine. But tomatoes don't grow well in San Francisco, on the other side of the San Francisco Bay, where there isn't enough sun. When we consider what to plant, we must account for the local climate, soil, and tall buildings. We still tend our garden vegetables, but instead of tomatoes we grow leafy greens.

Similarly, when we live together, we must take into account local conditions. Few Western churches make policy statements about polygamy, because a stance of monogamy may seem like a no-brainer.[9] By contrast, in Uganda,

7. Alves, *Protestantism*, argues that the Catholic Church does much better with tolerating a multiplicity of beliefs in its midst because it believes that salvation comes through the Eucharist. Because salvation is accomplished through the Eucharist—thus being included in God's people—minor disagreements are not as threatening to the church itself.

8. Armstrong, "How Many."

9. Interestingly, some non-Western Christians say that American Christians practice

where churches face the cultural reality of polygamous marriages, things get more complicated. Upon becoming a Christian, is a man to divorce all his wives but one? And how are those wives and children to support themselves? Similarly, a church in rural Kansas and urban San Francisco face different realities concerning homosexuality. The particular people and place where God plants us will shape our ethical concerns.

Seeking God's Grace Anew

Deciding how we are going to live together in the face of difficult moral questions will remind us that we are dependent on God's grace. We must seek the Spirit's guidance daily, rather than presuming that Christianity gives us the answer to every moral question in advance. As Dietrich Bonhoeffer says:

> The will of God is not a system of rules which is established from the outset: it is something new and different in each different situation in life, and for this reason a man must ever new examine what the will of God may be. The heart, the understanding, observation and experience must all collaborate in this task. It is no longer a matter of man's own knowledge of good and evil, but solely of the living will of God; our knowledge of God's will is not something over which we ourselves dispose, but it depends solely on the grace of God, and this grace is and requires to be new every morning.[10]

The debate over homosexuality gives us a chance to seek God's grace anew as local congregations confer with one another and ask, "Given this people, this place, and this time, how do we do God's will in regard to sexual minorities in our church and neighborhood?"

One congregation may see itself as a prophetic voice against the cultural idols of romantic love and self-fulfillment. As part of that vision it might choose to take the traditionalist stance. But then, by paying attention to the people in their midst and noticing the loneliness and alienation of LGBT members, it might undertake the practices of sacrificial love toward them.

Another congregation may realize the ways the church has self-righteously hurt LGBT people. It might choose to express its repentance for the sins of the church by adopting an affirming stance. But then, by paying attention to the people in its midst and noticing how modern culture does little

---

serial polygamy. Given all the divorce in our churches, they contend that we have multiple spouses, but have them one at a time.

10. Bonhoeffer, *Ethics*, 41.

to support the faithful love that gays and lesbians need, it might find ways of encouraging a "traditional" commitment to covenant fidelity.

Or a congregation might try to allow both perspectives. I know an astonishing and refreshing woman in her eighties who is part of a historically traditionalist congregation and became very concerned about the pain her congregation was causing gays and lesbians through its stance. Wanting to respect the convictions of members on both sides of the issue, she proposed that the congregation form two support groups.

In one, Christians from the traditional position would walk alongside same-sex attracted members compelled by the traditional perspective, accompanying them in the pursuit of celibacy or marriage to someone of the opposite sex and providing encouragement, accountability, and friendship.

In the other support group, an "ally" group, Christians from the affirming position would support gays and lesbians by offering social support as they seek same-sex romantic relationships, and by encouraging them to integrate life as a sexual minority with Christianity.

The congregation is actively considering this proposal and remarkably, its members are warming to the idea that their most important witness may not be divining God's will for all time on this issue, but rather figuring out how to live in love with one another in spite of real differences. They are striving to embody the grace that God so freely gives.

Revolutionary Subordination

Many Christians can't simply "go local" because the Catholic Church and many Protestant denominations are structured so that each local congregation has the same standards about ordination requirements, who can marry whom, and what constitutes the sacrament of marriage. How are Christians in these traditions to think about unity, particularly those who disagree with the official stance on same-sex relationships?

Because the debate is about a *non-essential* aspect of the Christian faith, it might be a good opportunity for individuals who disagree with the denomination's stance to practice what theologian John Howard Yoder calls revolutionary subordination.

Yoder looks at the difficult New Testament passages in which Paul counsels slaves to subordinate themselves to masters, and wives to husbands,[11] noting that such advice would not have been necessary in an ancient culture with its rigidly prescribed social roles *unless* slaves and women had been taught

---

11. 1 Pet 2:18–24, Eph 5:22–24, Col 3:18.

that they were free in Christ. Even though they were free, Paul and Peter counsel early Christians to subordinate themselves as a way of testifying to others. They were to imitate Christ's subordination to authority as a way of incarnating the way of Christ to those closest to them.[12]

In this light, subordination does not mean cowardly submission, nor a commitment to being "nice." Jesus said hard, truthful words and engaged in prophetic actions, such as cleansing the temple. But he did not abandon the people for whom he came. Given his confidence in God's redeeming action, Jesus subordinated himself to the leaders of his people. He recognized the authority of those over him, and when he prophetically witnessed against their wrongdoing, he accepted the consequences. Jesus *subordinated* himself to others, but he did not always *submit* himself to others.

In a modern age characterized by a commitment to the values of FIRE (freedom, individualism, rights, equality), such advice seems foolhardy. We're more inclined to demand others agree with us—and if they don't change their minds quickly, then leave.

But what does it mean, in the language of Romans 12:5, to be "members of one another"? How are people going to change unless those with different opinions bear with them, persevere, and through words and actions, present a better way? If we can't manage a unity even in the non-essentials of our faith, how are we ever going to move toward a visible unity that witnesses to the world that Christ has come?

For some people, living in such tension would be unbearably painful. Obviously, a gay couple may not be able to remain in a congregation in which gay relationships are denounced and a lesbian who remains celibate by conviction may not be able to stay in a congregation that celebrates same-sex relationships. But if we're ever going to be the diverse lot of people the New Testament envisions, then most of us will need to find ways to bear with and love people of differing cultures, economic backgrounds, and opinions on social issues.

As D. A. Carson reminds us:

> The church itself is not made up of natural "friends." It is made up of natural enemies. What binds us together is not common education, common race, common income levels, common politics, common nationality, common accents, common jobs, or anything else of that sort. Christians come together, not because they form a natural collocation, but because they have all been saved by Jesus Christ and owe him a common allegiance.[13]

12. Yoder, *Politics*, 162.

13. Carson, *Love*, 61.

"That the World May Believe"

John Howard Yoder suggests that unity of church government or doctrine, while important, is not unity "in Christ."[14] That is, hierarchies and doctrine are not the members of the church, but rather rich and poor, black and white, liberal and conservative, gay and straight.

For the disparate members of Christ's church to be knit together into a visible unity, as Christ prayed before he journeyed to the cross,[15] each of us will need to go through the difficulty of relating to people who are not like us. This will mean engaging in difficult conversations over the back fence, over coffee, and in the church foyer, talking about the most controversial topics in the company of the most convinced.

Though this may seem crazy, when we depend on God's grace, we invite the Holy Spirit to show up. Without God's grace, unity is clearly beyond us. We must have *faith* that, above all, we are brothers and sisters in Christ, *faith* that the Holy Spirit will honor Christ's prayer for unity, *faith* that God can redeem "impossible" situations.

Faith is the hope of what we do not see. Faith is not certainty—but what God asks of us, "so that the world may believe."[16]

Questions for Discussion

1. Why is it important to distinguish between "essentials" and "non-essentials" in the Christian faith? How might it be possible for the church to allow "liberty" in "non-essentials"? What would it mean to practice "charity in all things"?

2. Can you think of Christians who are different than you, either in your own congregation or elsewhere, who you could dialogue with (about homosexuality or something else) for the sake of church unity?

Other Questions from this Chapter

1. How is God at work in this conflict?

2. How can we cooperate in the midst of this conflict?

14. Yoder, *Royal Priesthood*, 291.

15. "That they [Christians] may all be one. As you, Father, are in me and I am in you, may they also be in us, so that the world may believe that you have sent me" (John 17:21).

16. John 17:21.

3. What might we learn from this conflict about church unity and being one in Christ?

4. If Christ's prayer were answered, how do you imagine that his church would practice the faith it professes?

16

Receiving the Kingdom

"It is only completely in this world that one learns to have faith. One must completely abandon any attempt to make something of oneself, whether it be a saint, or a converted sinner, or a churchman (a so-called priestly type!), a righteous man or an unrighteous one, a sick man or a healthy one. By this-worldliness I mean living unreservedly in life's duties, problems, successes and failures, experiences and perplexities. In so doing we throw ourselves completely into the arms of God, taking seriously, not our own sufferings, but those of God in the world—watching with Christ in Gethsemane. That, I think, is faith; that is metanoia; and that is how one becomes a man and a Christian."

—Dietrich Bonhoeffer

At one point in my life I had a clear picture of what faith would accomplish in my life: it would make me straight, get me a wife, and help me fit in. By God's grace I failed at all of these hopes.

As I failed it made me ask the question, "If God isn't giving me those things, what is God actually offering?" The answer has been a something like, "Do not be afraid little sheep, for it is your Father's good pleasure to give you the kingdom" (Luke 12:32, paraphrase).

Ironically, I didn't even know I wanted the kingdom. A friend of mine, Jeremy Alder, writes "Imagination and desire are fundamental. That's where the real work is to be done, the true battles waged."[1] Although I didn't know

---

1. Facebook post.

how or where to do battle for my life, God redirected my wants and desires toward God's extravagant hope for the world, and in the process grew my imagination.

Sexual desire has loomed large for me, and as I've wrestled with it, I've realized that I'm not mostly, as Western thought would have it, a rational animal with a big brain. I am, in theologian James K. A. Smith's words, one of God's erotic creatures "oriented primarily by love and passion and desire."[2] I am, as the Hebrews knew us to be, a yearner, a wanter, a knower, a faither.

Although I've been critical of the conservative evangelical tradition in which I grew up, this tradition did give me the gift of questioning my desires and helping me understand that some of my desires miss the mark.

There are moments when all I desire is a romantic relationship with a good man. But as enticing as I find that thought, I realize I want more. As a young Christian I hoped my sexual desire could point me to God, but my imagination was constricted and sterile because I thought I needed to love a God who was obsessed with me "getting it right."

My journey has helped me imagine a God who is an erotic being[3]—a God who wants me and wants to make love to a world suffering all of its spiritual, economic, social, and political pain.

In the midst of the pain, Jesus' message is that goodness is afoot and God is at work. I can turn from my own agenda, join God, and become God's lover, for the good of the world. Loving God is not a process of trying to work up affectionate feelings for an abstract, moralistic, invisible other. Just as God thought it was good for Adam to have a partner, so, too, God is looking for partners and helpers in the ongoing work of blessing the world—and crazily enough, God has invited this queer one to be his.

Day to day this means I try to make a small household of believers a home. I make the coffee. We gather each weekday morning to pray from *Common Prayer: A Liturgy for Ordinary Radicals*. I care for Jack's widow and she cares for me. I cook dinner and shop for groceries. I study Scripture and try to preach it. I work my RN job, ride my bike to have lunch with my friend Matt, go to movies with Rick, and try to show up for our many guests. I try to love others and receive their love. I keep a gratitude list: today it has a total of 1,636 items.

As far as I can tell, taking Jesus seriously means trying to live into his kingdom in all kinds of ways. It means yearning for the right and left to come to a real unity with each other that respects differences of opinions and the

2. Smith, *Desiring*, 76.

3. I don't mean "imagine" in the sense of imaginary, but rather as having the capacity to conceive of something.

people who hold them. It means getting beyond the "right" answer, beyond the idea that Christianity is mostly a morality hotline. It means striving for a new society beyond the most daring dreams of the Republican or Democratic parties.

It means working for a society called the church that is known for its love and unity, where "brother" and "sister" share what they have and lay down their lives for one another, serving and blessing one another and the world. It means celebrating the kingdom feast and enjoying it loudly enough so others hear of it and join in.

The conflict around same-sex relationships can either cause further division within the church, or, by faith, we can see the struggle as our teacher. By bringing up questions about family, social relations, church unity, and politics, this debate can help us think well and live more deeply into the dream God has for us and the world. It can help us, as God's little flock, receive the kingdom that God is offering with so much pleasure.

And if that happens, it will mean more gospel, more good news for everyone.

Questions for Discussion

1. What difference does it make to see yourself as a "yearner, a wanter, a knower, a faither" rather than as "a rational animal with a big brain"?

2. Given the curriculums in your life, how might they form your vocation? How is God inviting you to be God's loved partner for the sake of blessing the world?

Bibliography

Albert, Nathan. "I Hugged a Man in His Underwear. And I Am Proud." It Seems to Me
. . . Random Ramblings and Observations on Life. http://naytinalbert.blogspot.
com/#!/2010/06/i-hugged-man-in-his-underwear-and-i-am.html.

Alexander, John F. *The Secular Squeeze: Reclaiming Christian Depth in a Shallow World.*
Downers Grove, IL: InterVarsity, 1993.

Alison, James. "'But the Bible Says . . .'? A Catholic Reading of Romans 1." James Alison
Theology Blog. http://www.jamesalison.co.uk/texts/eng15.html.

Alves, Rubem A. *Protestantism and Repression: A Brazilian Case Study.* Maryknoll, NY:
Orbis, 1985.

"Anita Bryant." Wikipedia. http://en.wikipedia.org/w/index.php?title=Anita_Bryant&
oldid=583411957.

Apperson, G. L. *The Wordsworth Dictionary of Proverbs.* Ware, UK: Wordsworth, 1993.

Armstrong, Dave. "How Many Protestant Denominations are There? The 20,000–30,000
Numbers and David Barrett's Statistics." April 12, 2005. http://www.philvaz.com/
apologetics/a120.htm.

Armstrong, Kurt. *Why Love Will Always Be a Poor Investment.* Eugene, OR: Wipf and
Stock, 2011.

Auden, W. H., and Edward Mendelson. "Purely Subjective." In *The Complete Works of W.
H. Auden,* vol. 2, 184–97. Princeton, NJ: Princeton University Press, 2002.

Bagemihl, Bruce. *Biological Exuberance: Animal Homosexuality and Natural Diversity.*
New York: St. Martin's, 1999.

Bass, Diana Butler. "Can Christianity Be Saved? A Response to Ross Douthat." The
Huffington Post. July 15, 2012. http://www.huffingtonpost.com/diana-butler-bass/
can-christianity-be-saved_1_b_1674807.html.

———. *Christianity after Religion: The End of Church and the Birth of a New Spiritual
Awakening.* New York: HarperOne, 2012.

Becker, Ernest. *The Denial of Death.* New York: The Free Press, 1973.

Bellah, Robert N., et al. *Habits of the Heart: Individualism and Commitment in American
Life.* Berkeley, CA: University of California Press, 1985.

Berry, Wendell. *The Art of the Commonplace: The Agrarian Essays of Wendell Berry.* Edited
by Norman Wirzba. Washington, DC: Shoemaker & Hoard, 2002.

———. *Jayber Crow: A Novel.* Washington, DC: Counterpoint, 2000.

———. *Sex, Economy, Freedom and Community: Eight Essays.* New York: Pantheon, 1993.

Bonhoeffer, Dietrich. *Ethics.* Edited by Eberhard Bethge. Translated by Neville Horton
Smith. New York: Macmillan, 1965.

Brown, Paige Benton. "Singled Out by God for Good." www.pcpc.org/ministries/singles/singledout.php.

Calvin, John. *Institutes of the Christian Religion*. Translated by Henry Beveridge. Peabody, MA: Hendrickson, 2007.

Campolo, Tony. "A Possible Compromise on the Gay Marriage Controversy." The Huffington Post. February 22, 2011. http://www.huffingtonpost.com/tony-campolo/a-possible-compromise-on-_b_826170.html.

Capon, Robert Farrar. *The Astonished Heart: Reclaiming the Good News from the Lost-and-Found of Church History*. Grand Rapids: Eerdmans, 1996.

Carson, D. A. *Love in Hard Places*. Wheaton, IL: Crossway, 2002.

Cavanaugh, William T. *The Myth of Religious Violence: Secular Ideology and the Roots of Modern Conflict*. Oxford: Oxford University Press, 2009.

Clapp, Rodney. *Families at the Crossroads: Beyond Traditional and Modern Options*. Downers Grove, IL: InterVarsity, 1993.

———. *A Peculiar People: The Church as Culture in a Post-Christian Society*. Downers Grove, IL: InterVarsity, 1996.

———. "Why the Devil Takes Visa." *Christianity Today*, October 7, 1996, 18–33.

Coakley, Sarah. "Best of '10: Rethinking Sex and the Church, Part 3." ABC Religion & Ethics (Australian Broadcasting Corporation). July 16, 2010. http://www.abc.net.au/religion/articles/2010/07/16/2955345.htm.

———. *God, Sexuality and the Self: An Essay "on the Trinity."* Cambridge: Cambridge University Press, 2013.

———. "Love in Time of Infidelity: Rethinking Sex and Celibacy." ABC Religion & Ethics (Australian Broadcasting Corporation). October 30, 2012. http://www.abc.net.au/religion/articles/2012/10/29/3621015.htm.

Cohn, Emily. "Cost Of Raising a Child Climbs to $235,000 for Middle-Income Families." The Huffington Post. June 14, 2012. http://www.huffingtonpost.com/2012/06/14/cost-of-raising-a-child-c_n_1597729.html.

"Daily Infographic: If Everyone Lived Like An American, How Many Earths Would We Need?" *Popular Science*. http://www.popsci.com/environment/article/2012-10/daily-infographic-if-everyone-lived-american-how-many-earths-would-we-need.

De La Torre, Miguel. *Out of the Shadows into the Light: Christianity and Homosexuality*. St. Louis: Chalice, 2009.

Dobson, James C. *Preparing for Adolescence*. Santa Ana, CA: Vision House, 1978.

Dostoyevsky, Fyodor. *The Brothers Karamazov*. Translated by Constance Garnett. Mineola, NY: Dover, 2005.

Douthat, Ross. "Is Liberal Christianity Actually the Future?" *The New York Times*. July 25, 2012. http://douthat.blogs.nytimes.com/2012/07/25/is-liberal-christianity-actually-the-future/.

East, Brad. "Friendship in a Fallen World: An Ecclesial Reflection on Homophobia and Societal Consensus." *Resident Theology Blog*. http://resident-theology.blogspot.com/2009/05/friendship-in-fallen-world-ecclesial.html.

Ellul, Jacques. *Living Faith: Belief and Doubt in a Perilous World*. San Francisco: Harper & Row, 1983.

Foucault, Michel. *The History of Sexuality*. Translated by Robert Hurley. New York: Vintage, 1990.

Fowers, Blaine J. *Beyond the Myth of Marital Happiness: How Embracing the Virtues of Loyalty, Generosity, Justice, and Courage Can Strengthen Your Relationship.* San Francisco: Jossey-Bass, 2000.

Fowl, Stephen E. *Engaging Scripture: A Model for Theological Interpretation.* Malden, MA: Blackwell, 1998.

Fretheim, Terence. "Genesis." In *The New Interpreter's Bible: General Articles and Introduction, Commentary, and Reflections for Each Book of the Bible, including the Apocryphal/Deuterocanonical Books.* Vol. 1. Nashville: Abingdon, 1994.

Gagnon, Robert A. J. *The Bible and Homosexual Practice: Texts and Hermeneutics.* Nashville: Abingdon, 2001.

Gallup. "Special Report: 3.4% of U.S. Adults Identify as LGBT." Gallup Politics. http://www.gallup.com/poll/158066/special-report-adults-identify-lgbt.aspx.

Gold, Mitchell, and Mindy Drucker. *Crisis: 40 Stories Revealing the Personal, Social, and Religious Pain and Trauma of Growing up Gay in America.* Austin, TX: Greenleaf, 2008.

Harmon, Steven R. *Ecumenism Means You, Too: Ordinary Christians and the Quest for Christian Unity.* Eugene, OR: Cascade, 2010.

Harn, Roger Van, ed. *Exploring and Proclaiming the Apostles' Creed.* Grand Rapids: Eerdmans, 2004.

Haskell, David George. "Nature's Case for Same-Sex Marriage." *The New York Times,* March 30, 2013.

Hauerwas, Stanley. *A Community of Character: Toward a Constructive Christian Social Ethic.* Notre Dame, IN: University of Notre Dame Press, 1981.

Hauerwas, Stanley, and William Willimon. *Resident Aliens: A Provocative Christian Assessment of Culture and Ministry for People Who Know that Something Is Wrong.* Nashville: Abingdon, 1989.

Hays, Richard B. *The Moral Vision of the New Testament: Community, Cross, New Creation: A Contemporary Introduction to New Testament Ethics.* San Francisco: HarperSanFrancisco, 1996.

Hellerman, Joseph H. *When the Church Was a Family: Recapturing Jesus' Vision for Authentic Christian Community.* Nashville: B. & H., 2009.

Hsu, Albert Y. *Singles at the Crossroads: A Fresh Perspective on Christian Singleness.* Downers Grove, IL: InterVarsity, 1997.

Humanae Vitae; Encyclical Letter Pope Paul VI, July 25, 1968. Washington, DC: United States Catholic Conference, 1968.

James Baldwin: The Price of the Ticket. Directed by Karen Thorsen. American Masters: Season 4, episode 4, 1989.

John, Jeffrey. *"Permanent, Faithful, Stable": Christian Same-sex Partnerships.* London: Darton, Longman & Todd, 2000.

John Paul II. *The Theology of the Body: Human Love in the Divine Plan.* Boston, MA: Pauline, 1997.

Kampen, Melanie. "Pride 2013: 'I'm Sorry' Event." Ortus Memoria. June 2, 2013. http://ortusmemoria.wordpress.com/2013/06/03/pride-2013-im-sorry-event/.

Kinnaman, David, and Gabe Lyons. *UnChristian: What a New Generation Really Thinks about Christianity—and Why It Matters.* Grand Rapids: Baker, 2007.

Klam, Matthew. *Sam the Cat and Other Stories.* New York: Random House, 2000.

Kluger, Jeffery, and Elizabeth Dias. "Does God Want You to Be Thin?" *Time Magazine*, June 11, 2012. http://healthland.time.com/2012/05/31/blessed-are-the-sleek-why-god-wants-you-to-be-thin/.

Knust, Jennifer Wright. *Unprotected Texts: The Bible's Surprising Contradictions about Sex and Desire*. New York: HarperOne, 2011.

Kraus, C. Norman. *On Being Human: Sexual Orientation and the Image of God*. Eugene, OR: Cascade, 2011.

Lohfink, Gerhard. *"Does God Need the Church?" A Series of Lectures by the Catholic Integrated Community in the City of Vienna, Vol. 1*. Bad Tölz: Publishing House of the Catholic Integrated Community, 1998.

———. *Does God Need the Church?: Toward a Theology of the People of God*. Collegeville, MN: Liturgical, 1999.

Marin, Andrew P. *Love Is an Orientation: Elevating the Conversation with the Gay Community*. Downers Grove, IL: InterVarsity, 2009.

McClendon, James W. *Systematic Theology, Vol. 1: Ethics*. Nashville: Abingdon, 2002.

McLaren, Brian D. "A 'Farewell, Brian McLaren' Moment, or Not." http://brianmclaren. net/archives/blog/i-read-recently-about-your.html.

Miller, Donald. *Blue Like Jazz: Nonreligious Thoughts on Christian Spirituality*. Nashville: Thomas Nelson, 2003.

"A Model Predicts That the World's Populations Will Stop Growing in 2050." ScienceDaily. http://www.sciencedaily.com/releases/2013/04/130404072923.htm.

National Bureau of Economic Research. "The Size of the LGBT Population and the Magnitude of Anti-Gay Sentiment are Substantially Underestimated." http://www. nber.org/papers/w19508.

"New Marriage and Divorce Statistics Released." Barna Group. https://www.barna.org/ barna-update/family-kids/42-new-marriage-and-divorce-statistics-released#. Up9z7cS1yM4.

"New Normal: Americans' Views of Homosexuality Have Changed." *Christian Century*, June 27, 2012, 9.

Nobile, Philip. "The Meaning of Gay: An Interview with Dr. C. A. Tripp." *New York Magazine*, June 25, 1979, 36–41.

O'Donovan, Oliver. *Church in Crisis: The Gay Controversy and the Anglican Communion*. Eugene, OR: Cascade, 2008.

Paris, Jenell Williams. *The End of Sexual Identity: Why Sex is Too Important to Define Who We Are*. Downers Grove, IL: InterVarsity, 2011.

Piat, Stéphane Joseph. *Céline, Sister Geneviève of the Holy Face: Sister and Witness of Saint Thérèse of the Child Jesus*. San Francisco: Ignatius, 1997.

"'Porn & Pancakes' Fights X-rated Addictions." CNN. April 06, 2007. http://edition.cnn. com/2007/US/04/04/porn.addiction/index.html.

Report of the American Psychological Association Task Force on Appropriate Therapeutic Responses to Sexual Orientation. American Psychological Association. Washington, DC: American Psychological Association, 2009.

Roberts, Christopher Chenault. *Creation and Covenant: The Significance of Sexual Difference in the Moral Theology of Marriage*. New York: T. & T. Clark, 2007.

Rolheiser, Ronald. *The Holy Longing: The Search for a Christian Spirituality*. New York: Doubleday, 1999.

Schulz, Kathryn. "On Being Wrong." TED Talks. March 2011. http://www.ted.com/talks/ kathryn_schulz_on_being_wrong.html.

Scroggs, Robin. *The New Testament and Homosexuality: Contextual Background for Contemporary Debate.* Philadelphia: Fortress, 1983.

Smith, Christian. *The Bible Made Impossible: Why Biblicism is Not a Truly Evangelical Reading of Scripture.* Grand Rapids: Brazos, 2011.

Smith, James K. A. *Desiring the Kingdom: Worship, Worldview, and Cultural Formation.* Grand Rapids: Baker Academic, 2009.

Solzhenitsyn, Alexander Isaevich. *From under the Rubble.* Translated from the Russian by A. M. Brock, et al. Boston: Little, Brown, 1975.

Stark, Rodney. *The Rise of Christianity.* San Francisco: HarperSanFrancisco, 1997.

Story, Louise. "Anywhere the Eye Can See, It's Now Likely to See an Ad." *The New York Times.* January 14, 2007. http://www.nytimes.com/2007/01/15/business/media/15everywhere.html.

Sullivan, Andrew. *Love Undetectable: Notes on Friendship, Sex, and Survival.* New York: Knopf, 1998.

Thiselton, Anthony C. *The First Epistle to the Corinthians: A Commentary on the Greek Text.* Grand Rapids: Eerdmans, 2000.

Timmerman, Tim. *A Bigger World Yet: Faith, Brotherhood, and Same-Sex Needs.* Lyons, CO: Bird Dog, 2011.

Wade, Nicholas. "Pas De Deux of Sexuality is Written in the Genes." *The New York Times.* April 9, 2007. http://www.nytimes.com/2007/04/10/health/10gene.html?pagewanted=all&_r=0.

Walter, J. A. *Sacred Cows: Exploring Contemporary Idolatry.* Grand Rapids: Zondervan, 1980.

Weed, Josh. "The Weed: Club Unicorn: In Which I Come out of the Closet on Our Ten Year Anniversary." The Weed: All Kinds of Real. http://www.joshweed.com/2012/06/club-unicorn-in-which-i-come-out-of.html.

Williams, Rowan. "The Body's Grace." In *Our Selves, Our Souls, and Bodies,* edited by Charles Hefling, 58–68. Boston: Cowley, 1996.

Wilson, Ken. *A Letter to My Congregation: An Evangelical Pastor's Path to Embracing People Who Are Gay, Lesbian and Transgender in the Company of Jesus.* Canton, MI: David Crumm Media, 2014.

Wilson-Hartgrove, Jonathan. *The Wisdom of Stability: Rooting Faith in a Mobile Culture.* Brewster, MA: Paraclete, 2010.

Winner, Lauren F. *Real Sex: The Naked Truth about Chastity.* Grand Rapids: Brazos, 2005.

Wright, N. T. *Christian Origins and the Question of God.* Minneapolis: Fortress, 1992.

———. *Jesus and the Victory of God.* Minneapolis: Fortress, 1996.

———. "Romans." In *The New Interpreter's Bible: General Articles and Introduction, Commentary, and Reflections for Each Book of the Bible, including the Apocryphal/Deuterocanonical Books.* Vol. 10. Nashville: Abingdon, 2002.

Yoder, John Howard. *The Jewish-Christian Schism Revisited.* Compiled by Michael G. Cartwright and Peter Ochs. Grand Rapids: Eerdmans, 2003.

———. *The Politics of Jesus.* Grand Rapids: Eerdmans, 1994.

———. *The Royal Priesthood: Essays Ecclesiastical and Ecumenical.* Edited by Michael G. Cartwright. Scottdale, PA: Herald, 1994.

———. *To Hear the Word.* Eugene, OR: Wipf and Stock, 2010.

Online Resources

www.orientedtofaith.com

Please see the above website for:

- Additional articles and videos for each chapter
- Practical suggestions for churches (and other groups) who want to have a conversation about homosexuality
- Stories from people who have already participated in such conversations
- Helpful book reviews, quotes, video clips, websites, and more

Acknowledgments

Writing does not come easy for me. When asked about it I've often quoted Ernest Hemingway, who said, "There is nothing to writing. All you do is sit down at a typewriter and bleed." There is no way this book would exist without the help and support of friends and family. My debt to so many is so great it is almost embarrassing.

Zoe Mullery urged to me write this book many years ago, provided wise feedback, and generally gets the "most encouraging" award. Thanks also to Shane Claiborne for pushing me to write this book and for writing the foreword. Jonathan Wilson-Hartgrove has provided endless encouragement, and his life is one of the reasons I remain a Christian.

Heather Munn taught me much about the extravagance of God's kingdom economy as she provided professional feedback for free. I'll be forever grateful for an initial conversation with her over dishes. I'm thankful for the help of professors Kelly Johnson and Lisa Lamb, who graciously agreed to review the manuscript and provided important feedback. Thanks to Caitlin Mackenzie and Susie Heo for their helpful revisions. I appreciate editor Michael van Mantgem's painstaking review of my writing. Karen Hollenbeck Wuest carefully held my words, and provided much of the in-depth editing that made my paragraphs concise and readable.

Christian Amondson's over the top love feels like a huge grace, and I'm super grateful that he persevered in the conversation about publishing. That Ian Creeger did the interior design is one of those kingdom of God joys that makes me think God is enjoying us more than we know.

I'm grateful for the editing help of Kristyn Komarnicki on the introduction as well has her zeal for goodness and justice, which she embodies so beautifully in an exuberant life of blessing. One of the great joys of my life is teaching an apprentice group at Sojourners, and members Rachel Evans,

Jody Beavers, Sage Johnson, Lee Kuiper, and Greg Shafer read through the manuscript carefully and gave me invaluable feedback.

The whole Church of the Sojourners crew make my life possible and help me dare to believe the promises of the kingdom. It is our life together that gives anything I say here integrity.

Thanks to friends Allan Chan, Matt Toney, Rick DiMicco, Jeremy Alder, Daniel Boettcher, and Colin Chan Redemer for making friendship real, for bearing with me, and for talking with me about the book. To Dan Easdale, for loving me at a particularly vulnerable time; you gave me the help to keep going. To the "Dear Friends" crew, Mark Scandrette, Tim Lockie, Keoke King, Daniel Kirk, and Paul Nix, thank you for helping me keep perspective.

To my two friends, "Kent" and "Don," who didn't want their real names used, thank you for friendship, for entrusting me with your stories, and may this book help clear the way for the day when you don't need to be anonymous.

Sister Julie, I regularly tell others I have the best sister in the world. Your life of love blesses me and so many others.

Finally to my parents . . . I wince at times thinking about how parts of this book must be difficult for you. But I hope that more than anything you see how you instilled in me a love for God and the Christian story that I continue to hang onto with all my life.

About the Author

Tim Otto has a Masters of Theological Studies degree from Duke Divinity School, worked as an RN on the AIDS ward at San Francisco General Hospital for fourteen years, continues to work in home health, and helps pastor a small intentional church community in San Francisco.

Made in the USA
San Bernardino, CA
17 June 2016